SECRET MUSEUMS

GEORGES DE LA TOUR
&
PASCAL QUIGNARD

Translated from french
by Barbara Wright

XVII
century

FLOHIC
– EDITIONS –

Tallemant des Réaux relates that Monsieur Duret, the most celebrated doctor of his day — physician in ordinary to Henri IV — had taken it into his head that fire was injurious to him. When he saw embers in the hearth he had water poured on them. He trembled at the sight of candles.

That was how the seventeenth century began. In 1600, in Paris, a man couldn't bear to be in the same room as a flame or a fire. In 1600, in Vic, a child of seven, standing in front of a baker's oven, did not know that he was going to devote his life to that: a tête-à-tête between man and himself, with the aid of a flame.

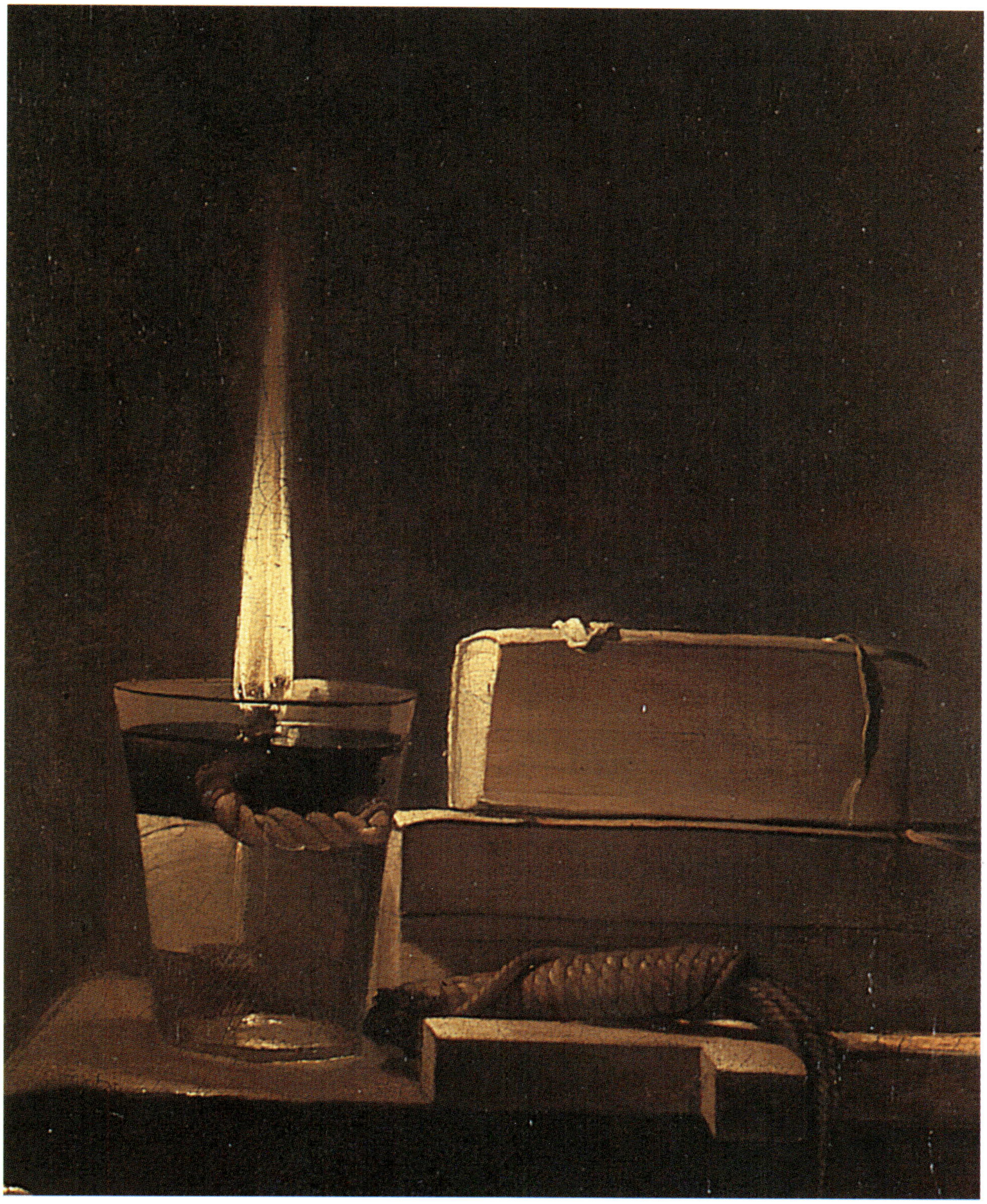

THE REPENTANT MAGDALENE
(known as Madeleine Terff).
Paris, Musée du Louvre
detail.

There have been two important candles in our history and they coincided in time: the lessons at Tenebrae in baroque music, and the candles in La Tour's paintings. The divine office of Tenebrae, during Holy Week, incorporated a rite in the course of which, one by one, accompanied by singing, the Hebrew letters that form the name of God were extinguished, and one by one a child in a red robe and a surplice blew out the candles representing them in the darkness of the agony. Jeremiah's *Lamentations* and Mary Magdalene's sighs were sung. Interspersed among the verses of the *Lamentations* there were vocalises sung on the Hebrew letters formed into an acrostic:

"*Aleph.* He hath led me and brought me into darkness
But not into light.
Beth. My flesh and my skin hath he made old.
He hath broken my bones.
He hath set me in dark places
As they that be dead of old."

Tomás de Victoria, Thomas Tallis, Marc Antoine Charpentier, Michel Lambert, Michel Richard Delalande, Couperin and Jean Gilles composed the most beautiful Tenebrae Lessons. In the first half of the seventeenth century there was at the same time a continuing renaissance and an immense wave of religion. This wave rose and grew from

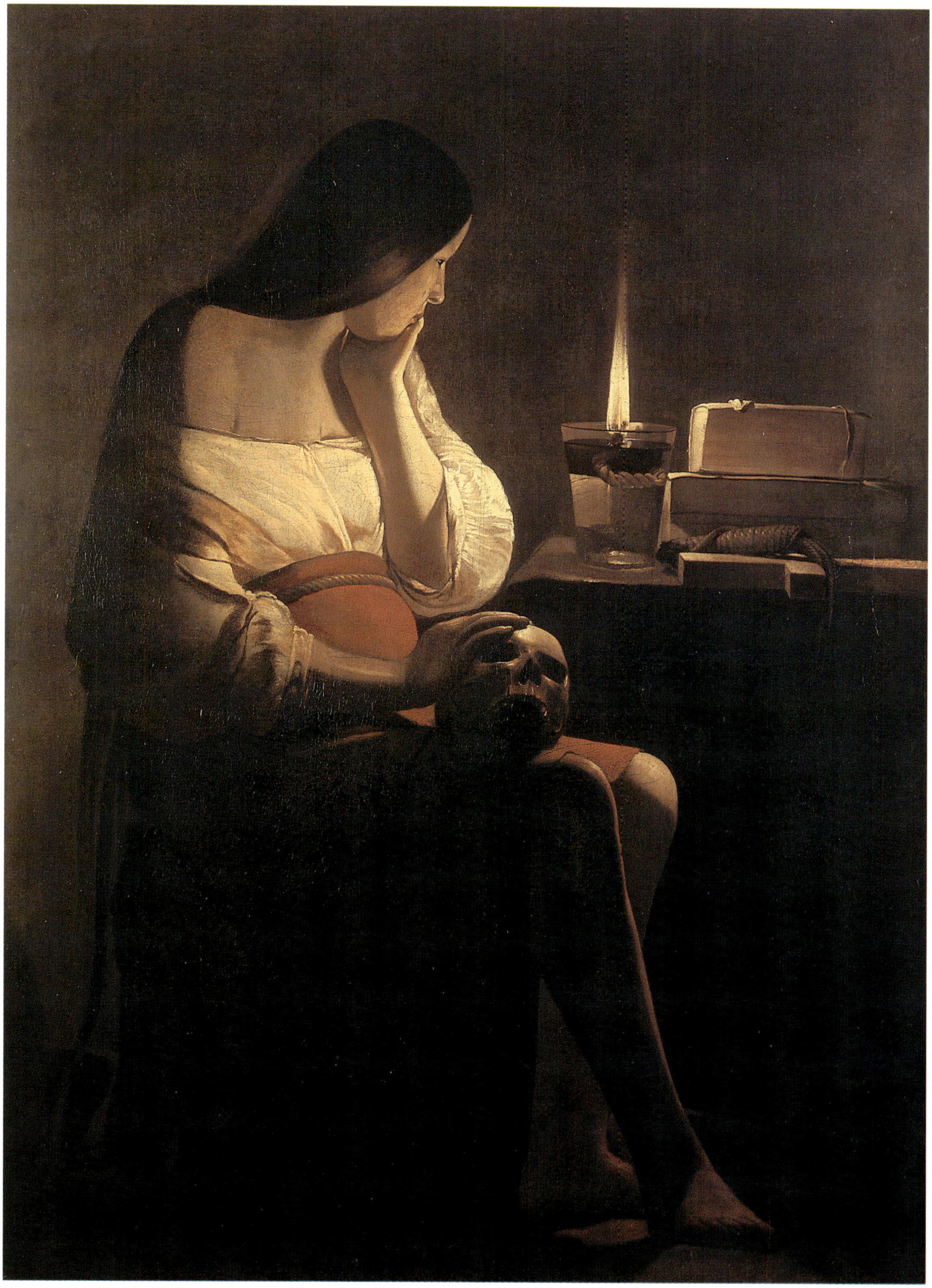

THE REPENTANT MAGDALENE
(known as Madeleine Terff).
Paris, Musée du Louvre
128 × 94 cm.

the end of the wars of religion until the death of Louis XIII, which is to say from 1594 to 1643, or even until the death of Mazarin in 1661. Georges de La Tour's images cannot be understood without Cardinal Bérulle, without the Abbé de Saint-Cyran, or without Jacques Esprit. They believed in the idea of a revival of the true initial piety, severe, ancient, pure, majestic. For the Counter-Reformation, the idea of the restoration of the Christianity of the first centuries was always combined with a reverie on primitive Rome.

La Tour made night into his kingdom. It is an interior night: a humble, enclosed dwelling in which there is a human body partly lit by a meagre source of light. The unity of the epiphany consists in: (1) the night, (2) the gleam of light, (3) the silence, (4) the enclosed dwelling, (5) the human body. A few strong principal colours, in comparison with which Le Nain seems cold, sad, green, grey. La Tour's oranges and reds burn beyond time, like glowing embers. A scene that is mere reportage in a painting by the Le Nain brothers, in La Tour becomes eternal. A brown mass, a lemon-yellow flame, a pure red, a cloudy vermilion, a sad grandeur. I am thinking of Racine's preface to *Bérénice,* which dates from 1670, in which he says that everything must be redolent of the "majestic sadness" that constitutes the pleas-

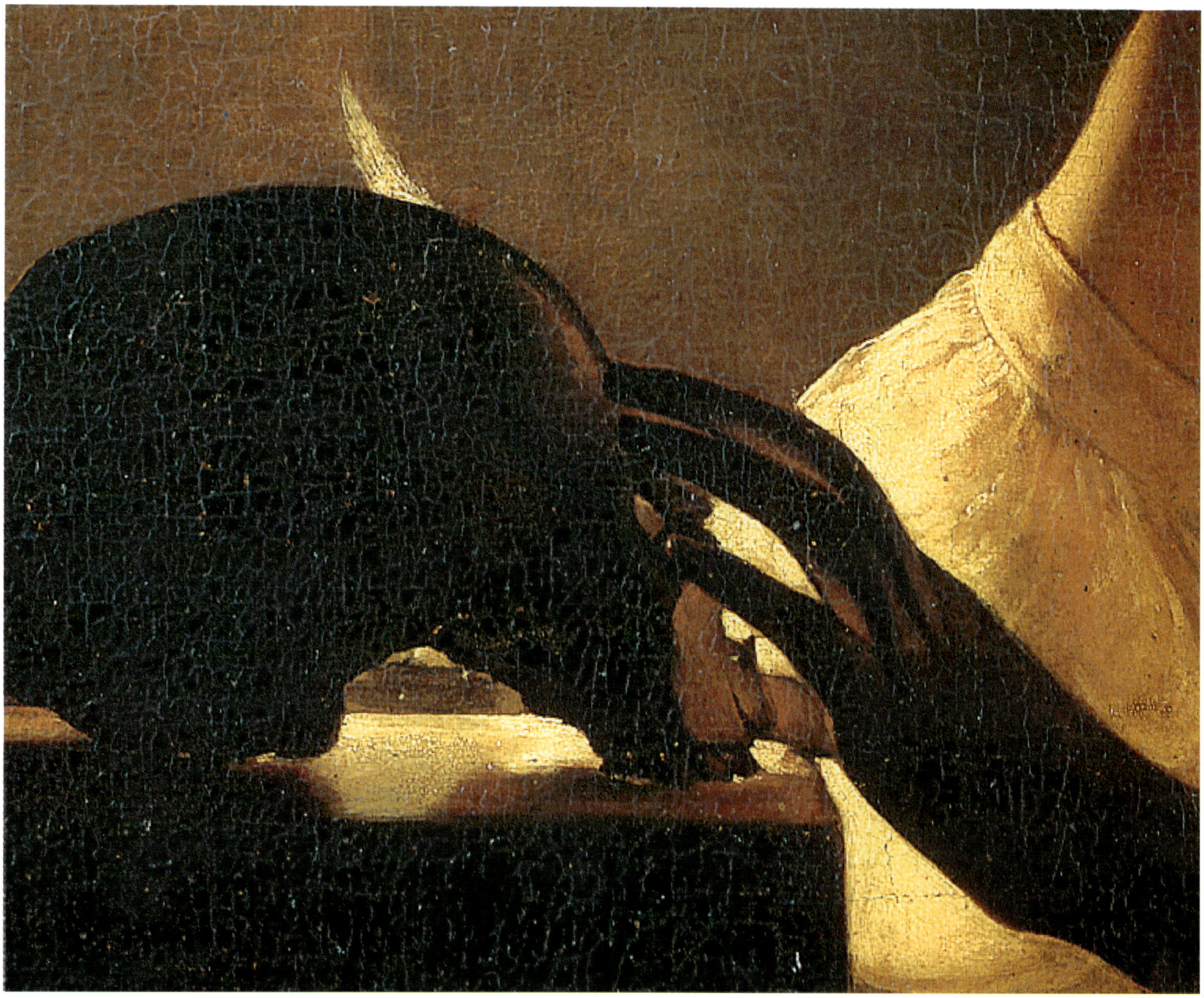

THE REPENTANT MAGDALENE
(known as Madeleine Fabius).
Washington, National Gallery
detail.

ure of tragedy. Louis Racine relates that his father, one day when he had taken La Fontaine to the Tenebrae service, saw that he was bored with the songs in the shadows and passed him a little Bible open at the page of Baruch's *Prayer of the Jews.* On the following days, Jean de La Fontaine would stop people in the street and ask: "Have you read Baruch? He was a great genius."

They were like the Vth century Greeks, and they knew it. The French genius is sublime and modest. Poussin, La Fontaine and Couperin did not assert themselves. La Tour was one of the last Renaissance geniuses. He rebelled against the painting of his day: against the sensual, decorative baroque of Simon Vouet, against the austere, scholarly classicism of Poussin. To contemplate a painting still had its old meaning for him: to pray in front of a sorrowful image. His paintings were so many variations on the cross on which God is nailed on the night of Holy Saturday.

Georges de La Tour, even more than Philippe de Champaigne, represents the Jansenist baroque. He borrowed from Honthorst the trick of hiding the source of light behind an iron screen, a hand, a figure, a skull. He stages great Gothic images. A solidly-constructed scene condenses a situation into something so simple that it is transformed into a mysterious rebus. It is so full of itself that it

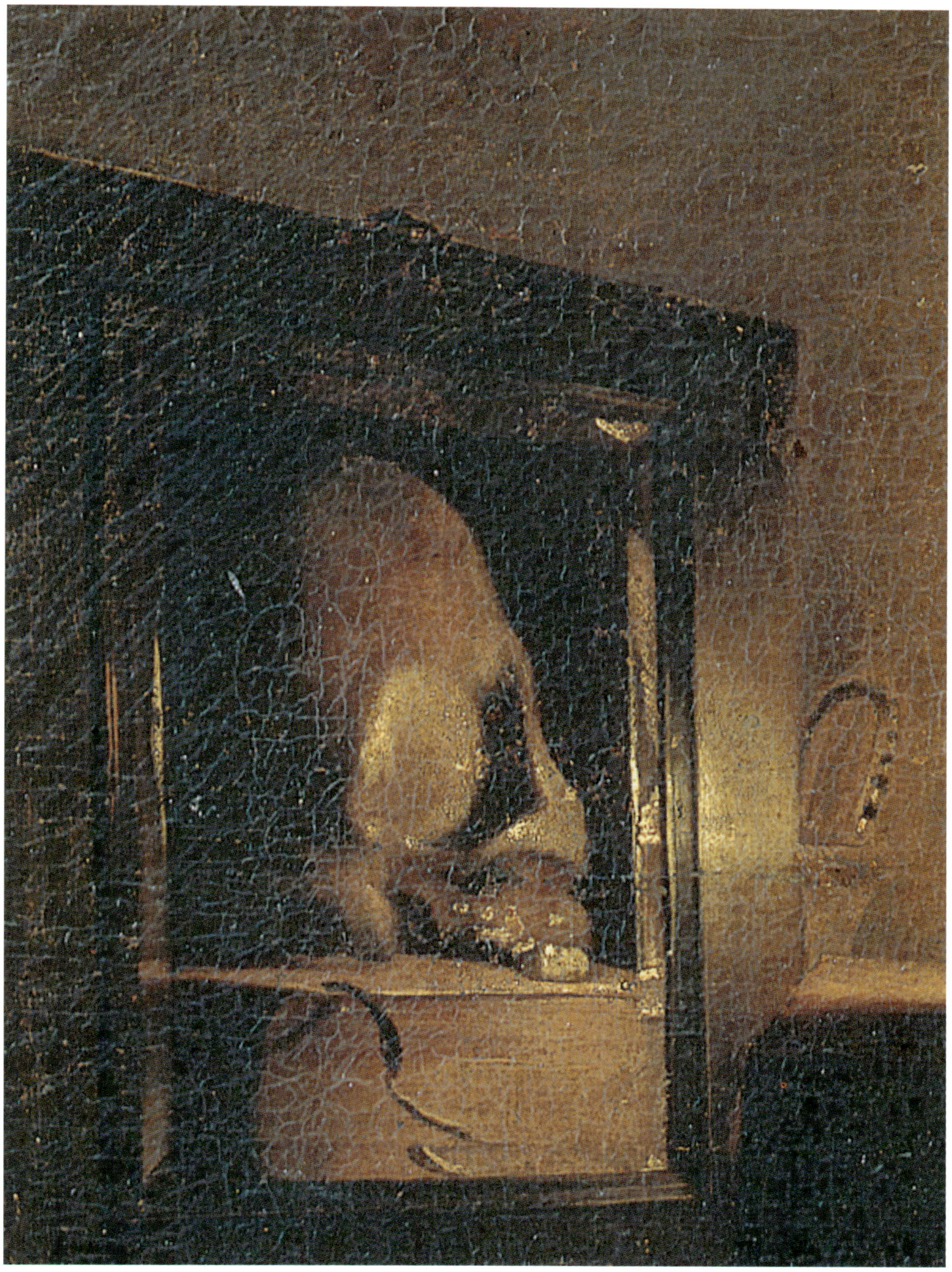

THE REPENTANT MAGDALENE
(known as Madeleine Fabius).
Washington, National Gallery
detail.

touches the edges of the frame, and culminates in a force of vision that is as influential as a gaze. And then the image becomes a trap in which the spectator — like the painter, no doubt — is caught. Through the representation of a birth, of a conversation between two men, of a woman dreaming, painter and viewer become one. It is in this sense that these silent paintings too are Tenebrae lessons; what François Couperin also was seeking was that "direct communication" which is the religion of the seventeenth century. Pierre Nicole said that holy images, in the form of fantasies, ought to be mental orisons that create an indissoluble link with God.

"Che silenzio!" exclaimed Bernini, when shown Poussin's paintings. With La Tour, the Word itself is in his night. Silence has become the Passion of silence. It is the last silence.

I

One winter's day, a baker named Jean took his son in his arms. The river Seille was covered in ice. Round the baptismal font on March 14, 1593 were Jean de La Tour, his wife Sibylle Molian, the granddaughter of a baker, the wife of the Vic

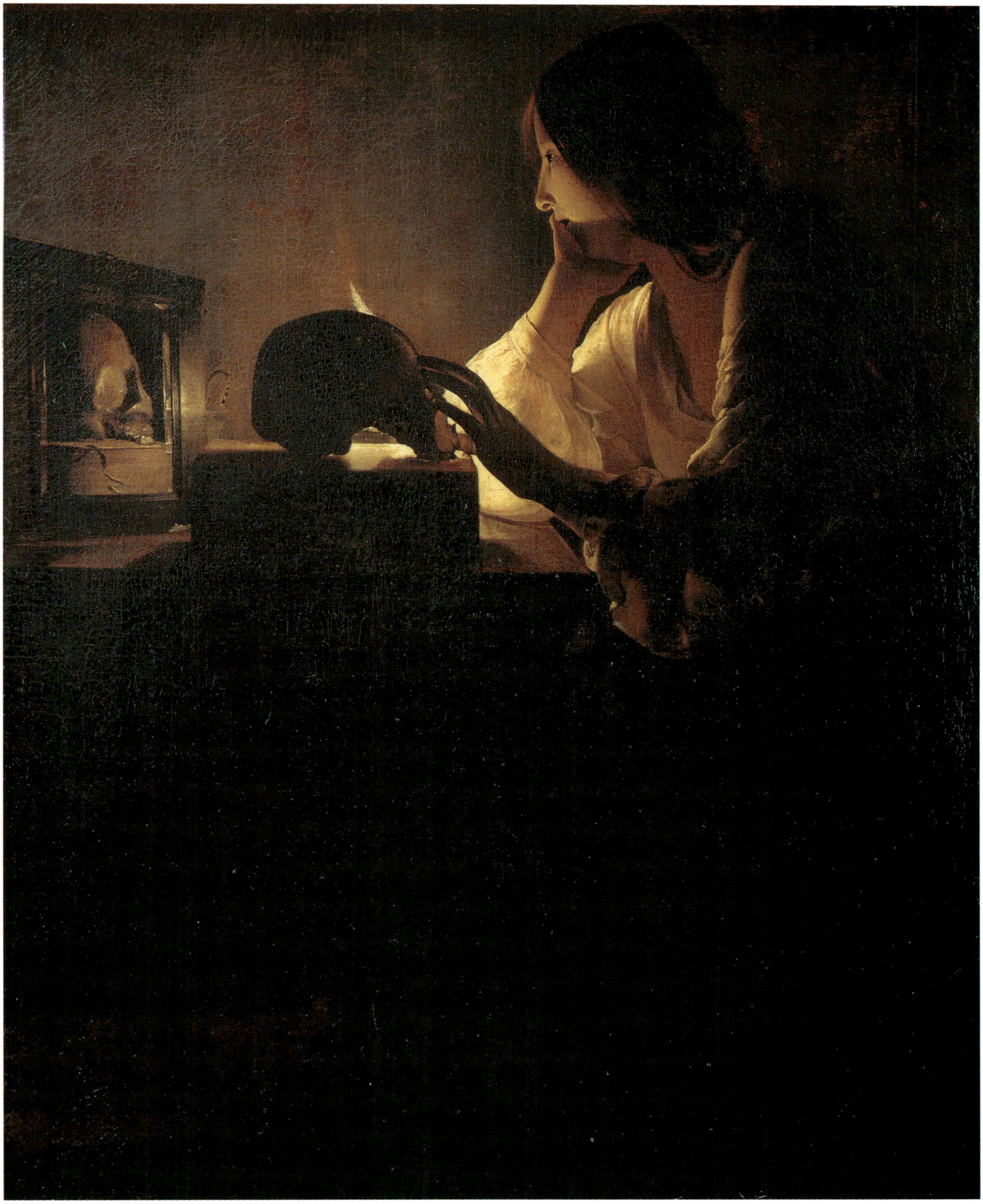

THE REPENTANT MAGDALENE
(known as Madeleine Fabius).
Washington, National Gallery
113 × 93 cm.

miller, and the draper. Jean de La Tour and his wife had seven children. Georges was the second. They lived in a little house on the banks of the Seille, near the church. The family spoke mainly French, and a little German.

It is not known who his masters were, nor what countries he visited. Like François Couperin, like Pierre Nicole, like Jacques Esprit, he was soon forgotten.

There is no certainty about the titles of Georges de La Tour's paintings. Except for a page in an account book which refers to "Image Saint Alexis." It was Charles Sterling who suggested calling two paintings by Georges de La Tour "Magdalen with a Night-Light" and "Magdalen with a Mirror." Paul Jamot has commented on the *Magdalen with a Mirror* and stressed the audacity of the immense black mass that occupies the whole of the lower part of the picture; the light is concentrated only on the face, the bust, the hesitant hand and the long fingers lightly touching and endeavouring to grope their way towards a recognition of the contours of death.

The skull masks the light. The tip of the flame flickers slightly in the breath of the woman possessed by seven evil spirits who sighs in front of an empty skull, which represents our mental picture of our destiny.

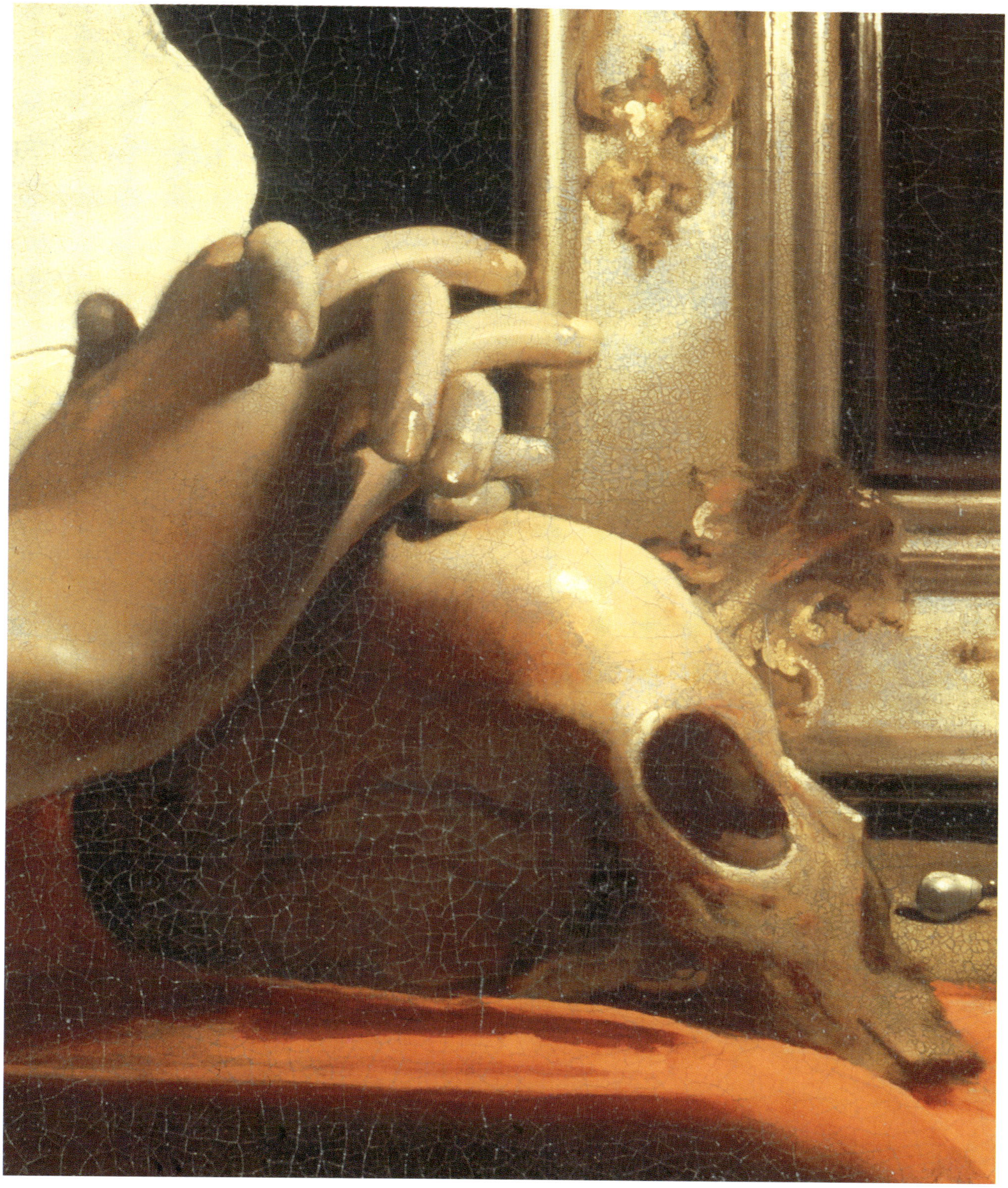

THE REPENTANT MAGDALENE
(known as Madeleine Wrightsman or Madeleine with two flames).
New York, Metropolitan Museum
134 × 92 cm.

Paul Jamot, writing of the *Magdalen with a Night-Light,* regretted that the light had to be turned on to the Magdalen's legs. "The bare legs are not a happy thought." It is true that they are neither sensual nor attractive; they are awkward, unexceptional, strange and simple. Modesty, wrote Jacques Esprit, is "an embellished approach." It is "economical ostentation." Through the silence of the painting, ordinary things are trying to become intensely ordinary. Georges de La Tour wanted the Magdalen's traditional ample, blonde, curly head of hair to become smooth and black. The traditional tears of the penitent do not run down her face. She is not a repentant Venus but a serious woman whose body has enjoyed pleasure, and who thinks. The seductress no longer looks at us men. Nor does she look directly at the death's-head. She looks at the reflection. It is not her own reflection. Every face is death. The other world is there in the dark waters of the mirror, which stands out like a door opening on to the other world.

There, where the Magdalen was expecting to see her own features, she sees the world of the dead, and its silence.

All the figures Georges de La Tour painted are immobile, divided between the darkness in which they appear and the gleam of light that partially

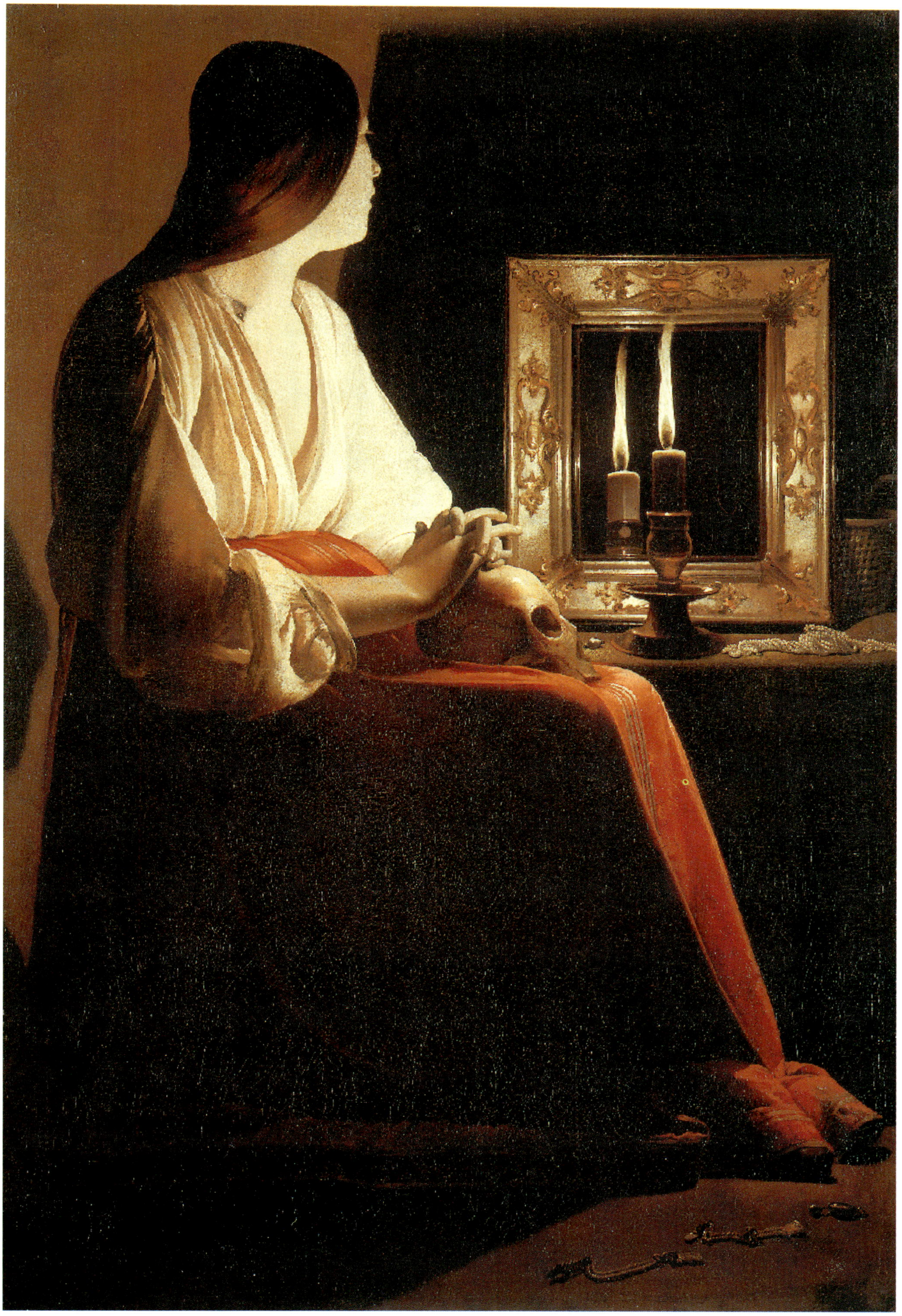

THE REPENTANT MAGDELENE
(know as Madeleine Wrightsman or Madeleine with two flames).
New York, Metropolitan Museum
detail.

illuminates them. Looming out of the shadows, touched by a glimmer of light, they are making an incomprehensible, suspended gesture. These bodies, seen from above, thereby gain the stature of idols. The very limited number of pigments and colours with which they are endowed enhances their appearance. The structure of these canvases and of the bodies that fill them is an enormous framework that intentionally impinges on the limits of the surface. Big patches of very solid, flat tints divide this surface. The volumes enclosed by the darkness, and the attitudes induced by immobility, are almost stiff, and tend to become geometrical. The extraordinary monochromy is due to the gleam of light. The most humble bodies become monuments, and make one think of the representation of gods. The details die: the shade and the jaws of death devour them. Everything becomes increasingly solemn and increasingly simple. Night simplifies us. Silence and the hour give shelter. The single source of light unifies.

The candle makes visible the place where it is exposed, but it cannot be said that it sees. It cannot be supposed that the people it illuminates realise that they are visible. They look neither at the light, nor at themselves, nor at the objects. With Georges de La Tour, the light reveals, without the knowledge of the bodies it is revealing. They are

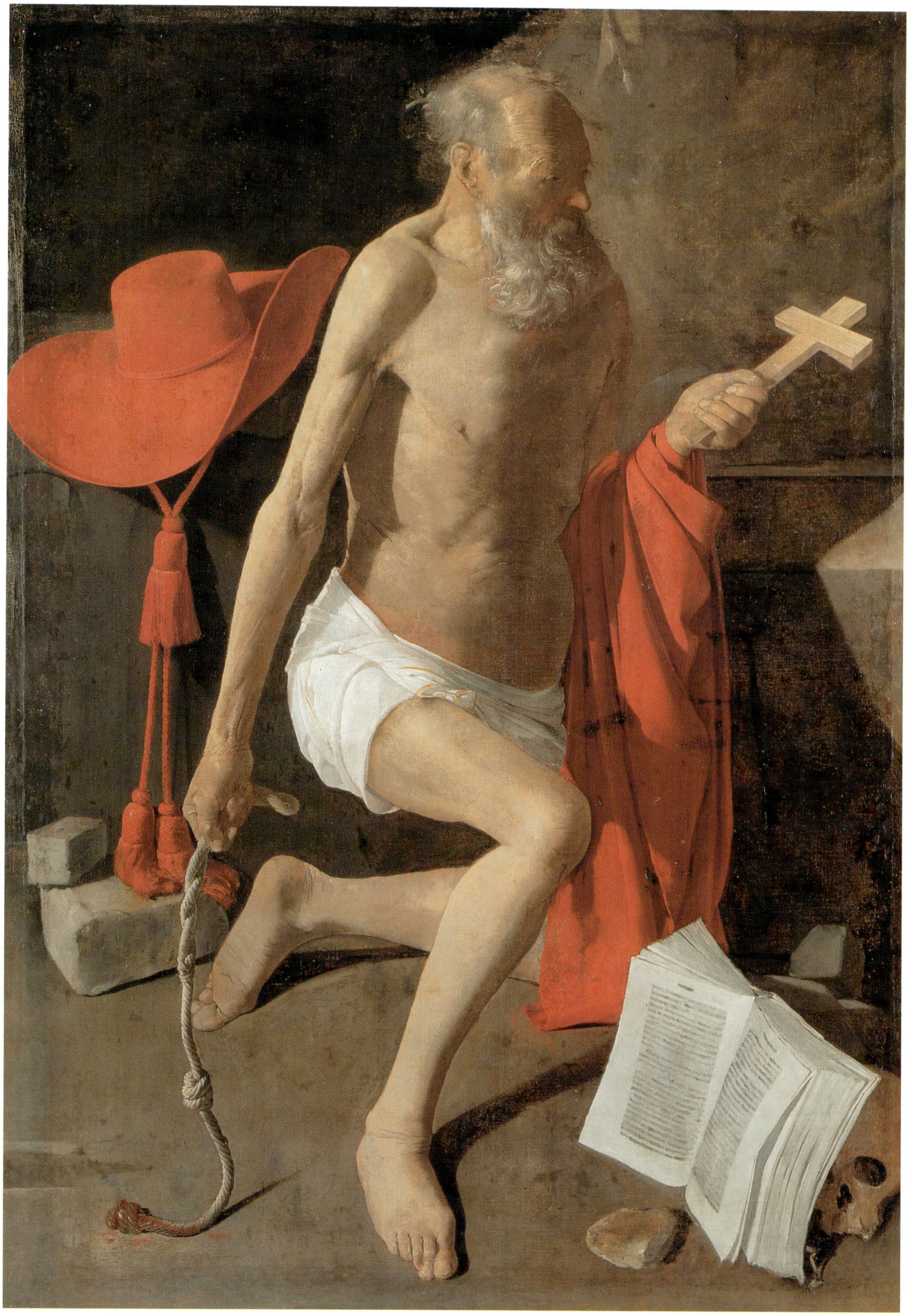

THE PENITENT SAINT. JEROME.
Stockholm, Nationalmuseum
153 × 106 cm.

caught unawares in a state of ecstasy; in a state of stupor; or insomnia; or fatigue; caught unawares in the undivided attention they devote to crushing a flea or a louse with their nails; caught unawares at the very moment they are blowing on a flame or on a lighted pipe, or on the charcoal stick they are holding between their fingers.

They do not speak to the people who see them. They do not look at the gleam of light that is illuminating them without their knowledge. They are absorbed by a thought. They take no part in our world. They are our life when we are in the other life, when we are no longer on display; when, undressed, just as we were thinking of going to bed, an empty thought, an inward look, makes us dwell on ourselves.

We are watching the loved one sleep.

It sometimes happens that we suddenly feel called to solitude. Even our love life unexpectedly generates sudden, panicky cravings for solitude. It is the wish to be alone, to do things without being watched. It's the wish to be able to relax our features, to remove our face. To tell the truth, it's sometimes simply the wish to have a bath or to cut our nails. The urge to be a hermit for an hour or two. The wish to cleanse one's heart in silence. To whisper our idleness and emptiness to ourself in the silence, and to soap ourself like a

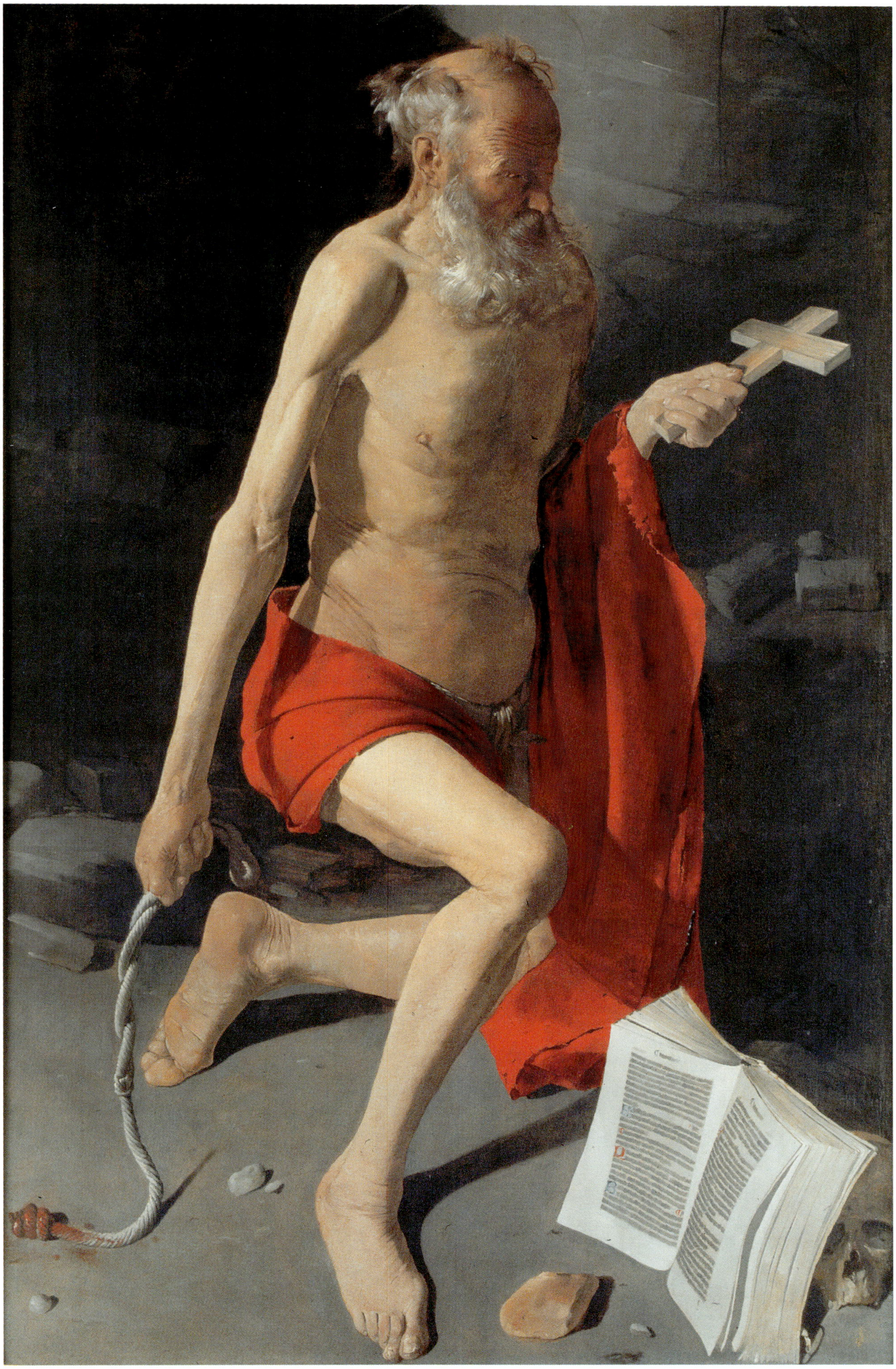

THE PENITENT SAINT. JEROME
(with halo).
Grenoble, Musée des Beaux-Arts
157 × 100 cm.

former baby.

When we have been unable to sleep and have got up to drink a glass of water, wandering through the darkened rooms, sitting down, lighting a cigarette, we think about the universe of sleep which we are not going to enter — and sometimes about the daylight which has disappeared. We do not think that the embers or the flame of a match are illuminating us for a moment. Or when we are getting ready to stand up again, when we are thinking of going back to bed, when we are worrying about the day to come, about the light to come, but which does not come, which will not come, as the dawn is so distant for someone whom insomnia keeps outside dreams and outside the daylight, then the silence of these paintings reigns in the room we are in.

We remain silent before our own life. We search for our history but we don't know what it is and we remain silent before its absence. All the figures who occupy these paintings are keeping silent before their own history. The child Jesus is a little boy who is waiting for his history. The young Mary is waiting for her history and remaining silent before it. Peter remains silent in the face of his betrayal. The Magdalen does penitence; calls on her recollections; bids farewell to her memories of sensuality; never ceases to bid farewell to the

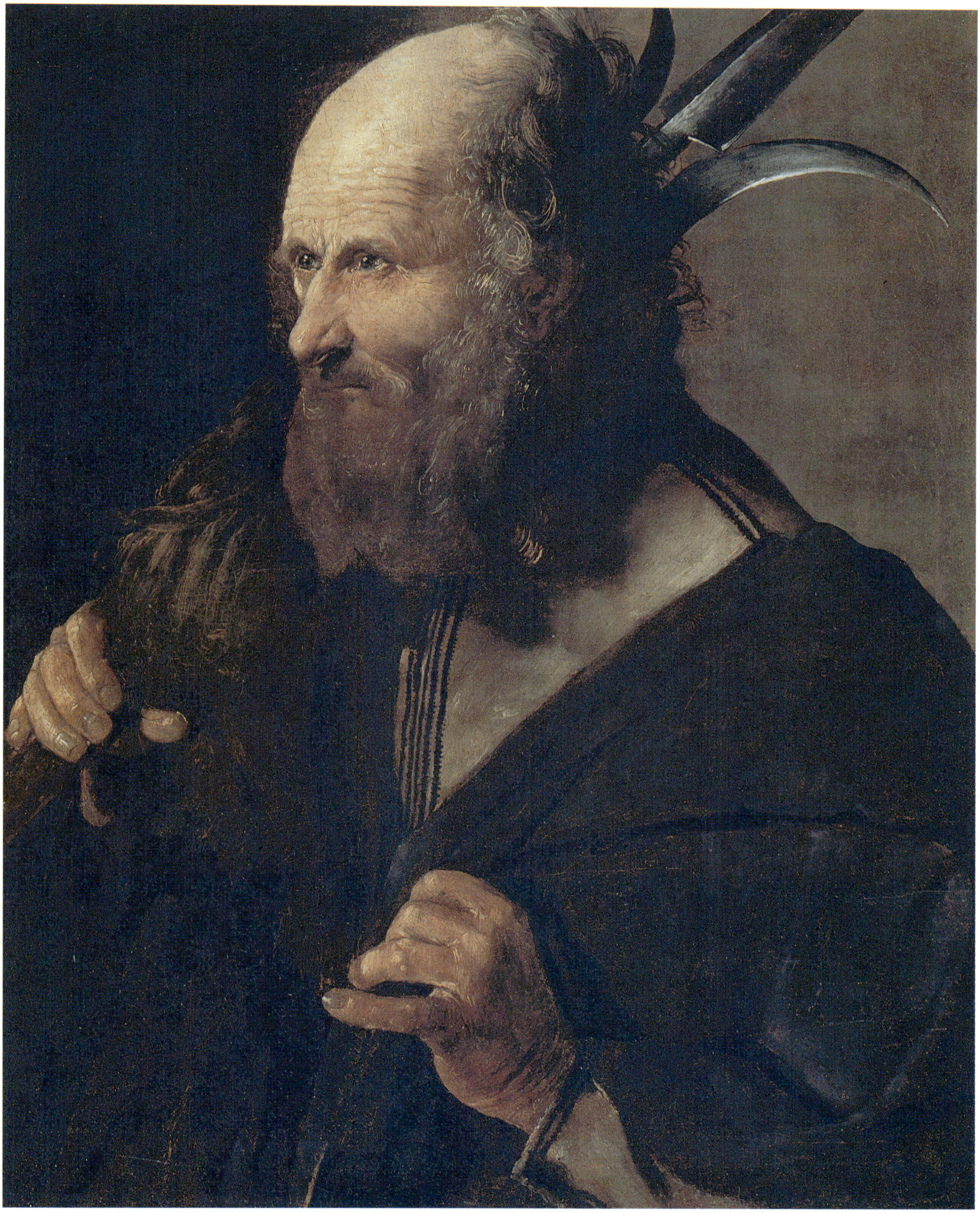

SAINT JUDE THADEE
(also mistakenly known as Saint Mathieu).
Albi, Musée Toulouse-Lautrec
62 × 51 cm.

phantasms that sometimes visit her. She says to her knees: "Farewell, my knees, you will not know the hands of a child clinging to the two bones jutting up in you, who climbs up, who settles himself, and whom one cradles.

"Farewell, my thighs, you will not press the loins of a man carried away by pleasure. You are useless envelopes.

"Farewell, my hands, you will no longer cut vegetables, you will no longer peel fruit, you will no longer pluck lettuces, you will no longer cook meals, you will no longer scrub clothes. You will no longer wash the dusty feet of the Lord. You will no longer insinuate yourselves tenderly between the fingers of a sighing man. You will no longer clasp each other round the big body that turns over and extends his lips to you in the dark.

"Farewell, my womb, you will no longer know men's rodlike organs. You will not know childbirth.

"Farewell, my breasts, the toothless mouths of infants will not suck you. Men's thick, bristly lips will no longer provoke you, or make you quiver."

II

Jansenism and the baroque Counter-Reformation were inner decisions that were more universal than

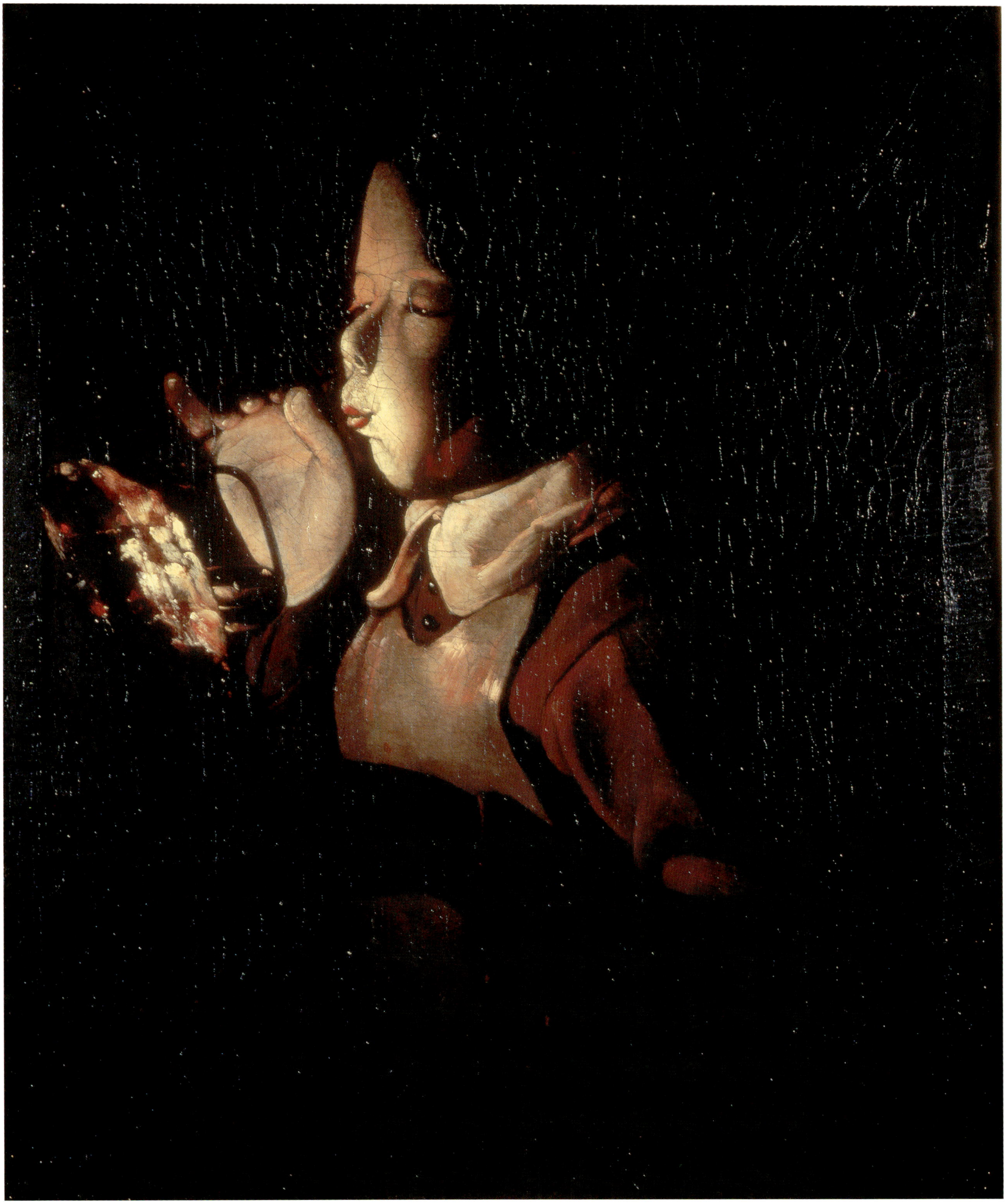

THE LAMP-BLOWER.
Dijon, Musée des Beaux-Arts (Granville)
61 × 51 cm.

the faith and its wars that spread them. And the work these periods produced, in Italy, England, Spain and France, have a far greater destiny than their time, or classical doctrine alone. Because their foundation is stupor in the face of death, which they describe as a thing in itself, and not the god who redeems it. Because time, abandonment, sexuality and death constitute the holy family that reigns over men without mercy and without respite.

Jacques Esprit was born on October 23, 1611 in Béziers. His was some of the most beautiful prose of the seventeenth century, and it was as unknown as was La Tour himself at the beginning of this century. Esprit lived as a parasite on Chancellor Séguier and Madame de Laval. During the Fronde, he attached himself to the Duchesse de Longueville. He followed her to Munster in 1649. He was subject to migraines so violent that they drove him mad. He sought treatment at the Oratory, where he met the Prince de Conti. Then he married a woman who complained that he had made her pregnant three times. He died in Béziers on July 6, 1678, when he was at last publishing his book, the two volumes of *The Falsehood of Human Virtue.*

He treated everything with scepticism. The thesis he defended is as simple as it is radical. La

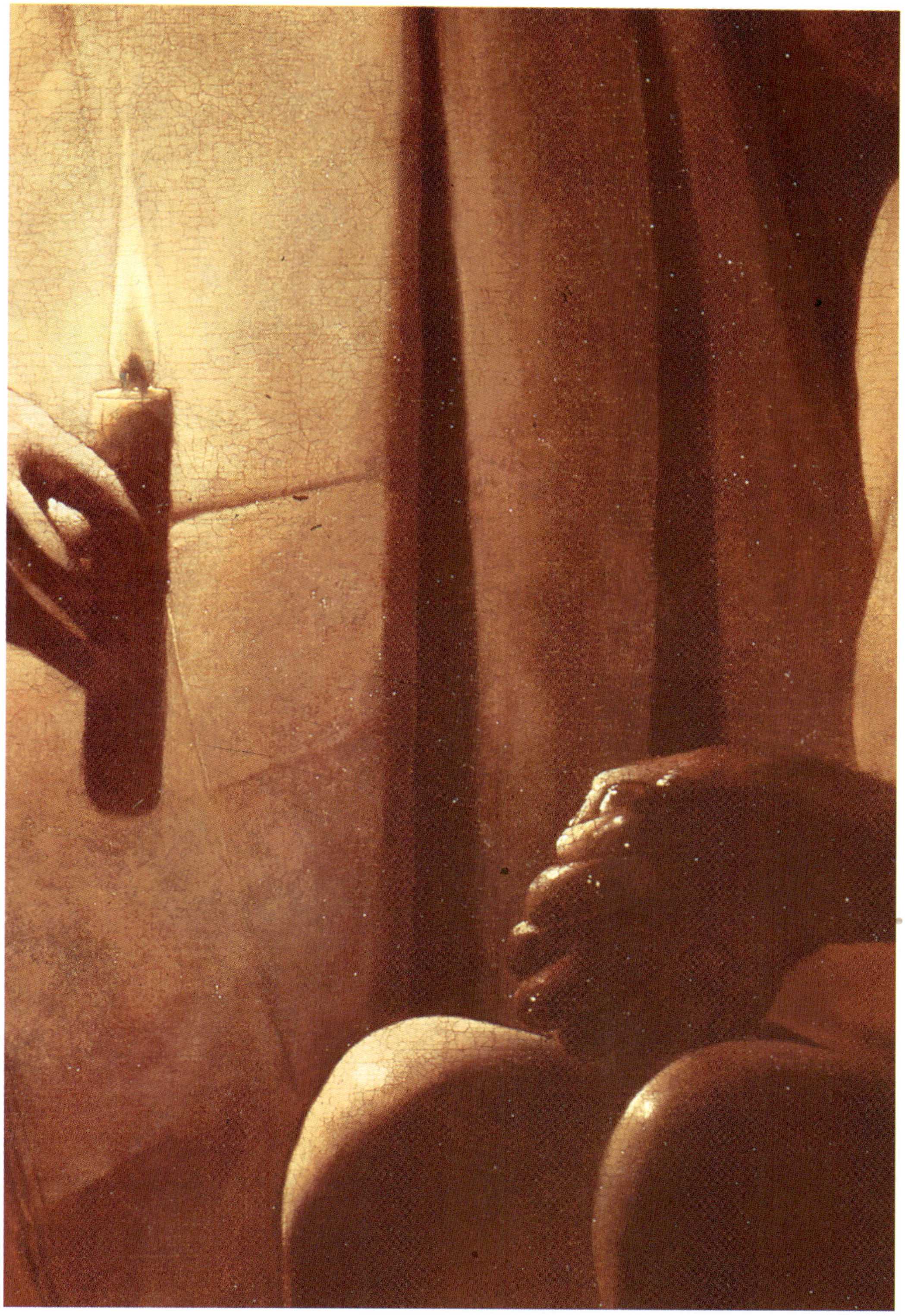

JOB AND HIS WIFE.
Epinal, Musée départemental des Vosges
detail.

Rochefoucauld, like the Jansenists, praised it and took inspiration from it. All men are enigmas, difficult to decipher. We are mistaken in our judgements. The most favourable hypotheses we put forward are the most unjust. Men's virtues are falser and more perverse than the vices they indulge in. Neither reason, nor goodness, nor justice, nor love, nor piety, nor generosity are as worthy sources of thought as they seem. No one is good willingly. The mind is always more vulgar than the body in its most humble functions. A hellish somnolence is lying in wait for us. The passion of the first sin caused everything in us to degenerate. Because of this tainted foundation and original darkness weighing upon us, our nature is permanently double. Covered by the veil of his senses, man perceives only the shadow of his true desire, and hastens towards the obscure, unsubstantial area that the sun or the flames leave behind both things and bodies. Being enemies of God and ungrateful and rebellious children, we cannot count on his grace, assuming that he should condescend to turn his eyes on to us. But there is nothing to assure us that God has pity, because he is so just, and this is something we must do for ourselves, as a vain consolation, in the darkness in which we are groping our way, wandering between abysses of inexistence.

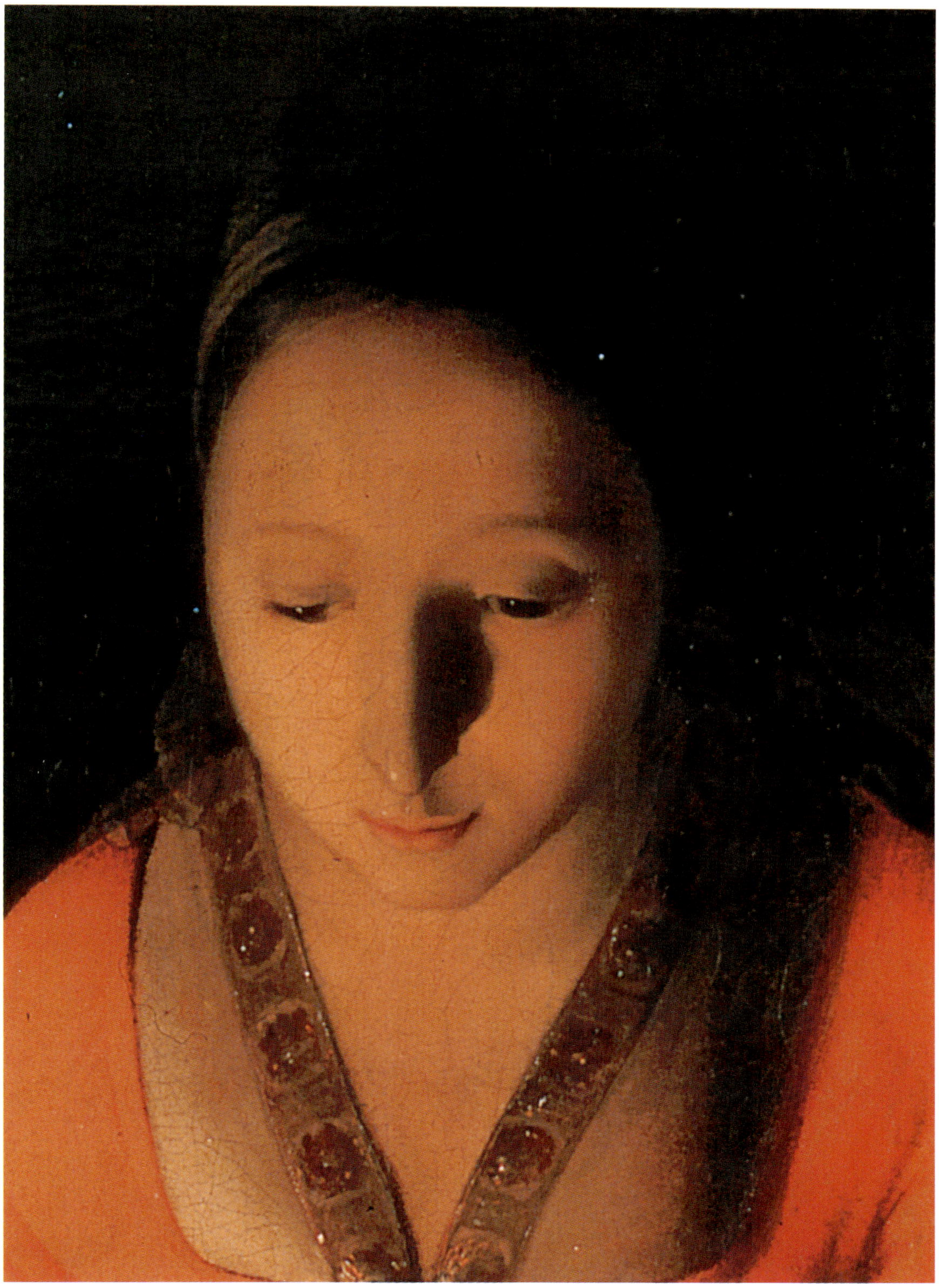

THE NEWBORN.
Rennes, Musée des Beaux-Arts
detail.

La Tour's paintings are images that are enigmas. An enigma is something we allow to be understood without saying it. This world is double. Saint John of the Cross believed in the doctrine of "Nadas": *The Ascent of Mount Carmel* proceeds by successive negations, and that is how we gradually enter the "Dark Night." Saint Teresa said that the Magdalen was still mortal when she discovered God. That it had been regrets followed by regrets. Saint John of the Cross used to repeat to the brothers: "The complete darkness of the dark night is the only dawn the soul can know."

Juan de Yepes, known as John of the Cross, died in Ubeda, in the province of Jaén, on December 14, 1591, at the darkest hour, midnight, at the age of forty-nine. The first edition of his books was published in Alcalá in 1618, with the exception of *The Spiritual Canticle.* The first edition of the *Canticle* was produced in Paris in 1622, in a French translation by René Gaultier. The first complete edition of John of the Cross was published in Madrid in 1630. John of the Cross was beatified in 1675. He was canonised in 1726.

Georges de La Tour chose the most simple everyday life, simplified it by plunging it into darkness, only to invest it with the "accidental light of grandeur" that comes from a gleam, a shaft of light. Which is the very source of the aureola, the

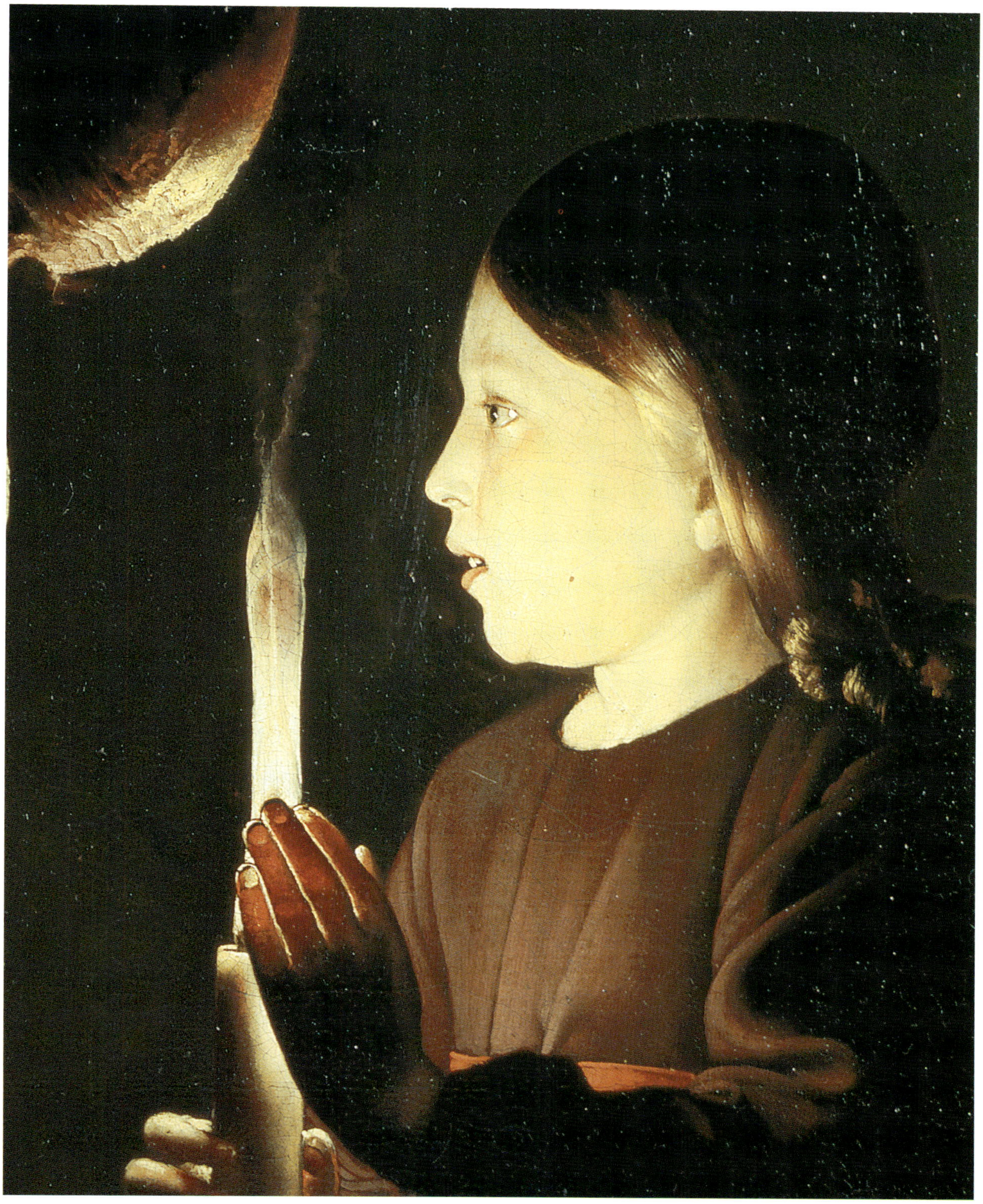

SAINT JOSEPH THE CARPENTER.
Paris, Musée du Louvre
detail.

haloes that consecrate. He obeyed Caravaggio's lessons. He sacrificed all the haloes that encircle the heads of gods and saints and substituted the glints of a candle.

John of the Cross's doctrine of "Nothingnesses" makes this recommendation for the attainment of simplicity: "You should have an equal love for and an equal forgetfulness of all persons, whether relatives or not, and withdraw your heart from relatives as much as from others, and in some ways even more, for fear that flesh and blood might be quickened by the natural love which is ever alive among kin and kith... Regard all as strangers... Do not love one person more than another, for you will err." John of the Cross's parents were weavers of silk toques, and were in reduced circumstances. John's elder brother, Francisco de Yepes, who was also a silk weaver, said they ate barley bread more frequently than wheaten bread, and even very little of that. As children they used to beg, because their father was dead. Francisco de Yepes said that they did not possess two candles: John used to go into a woodshed to read at night by the light of the only candle. As an adolescent he tried the trades of engraver and painter, but was not taken on as an apprentice. There still exist drawings by John of the Cross of Christ Crucified, and of Mount Carmel.

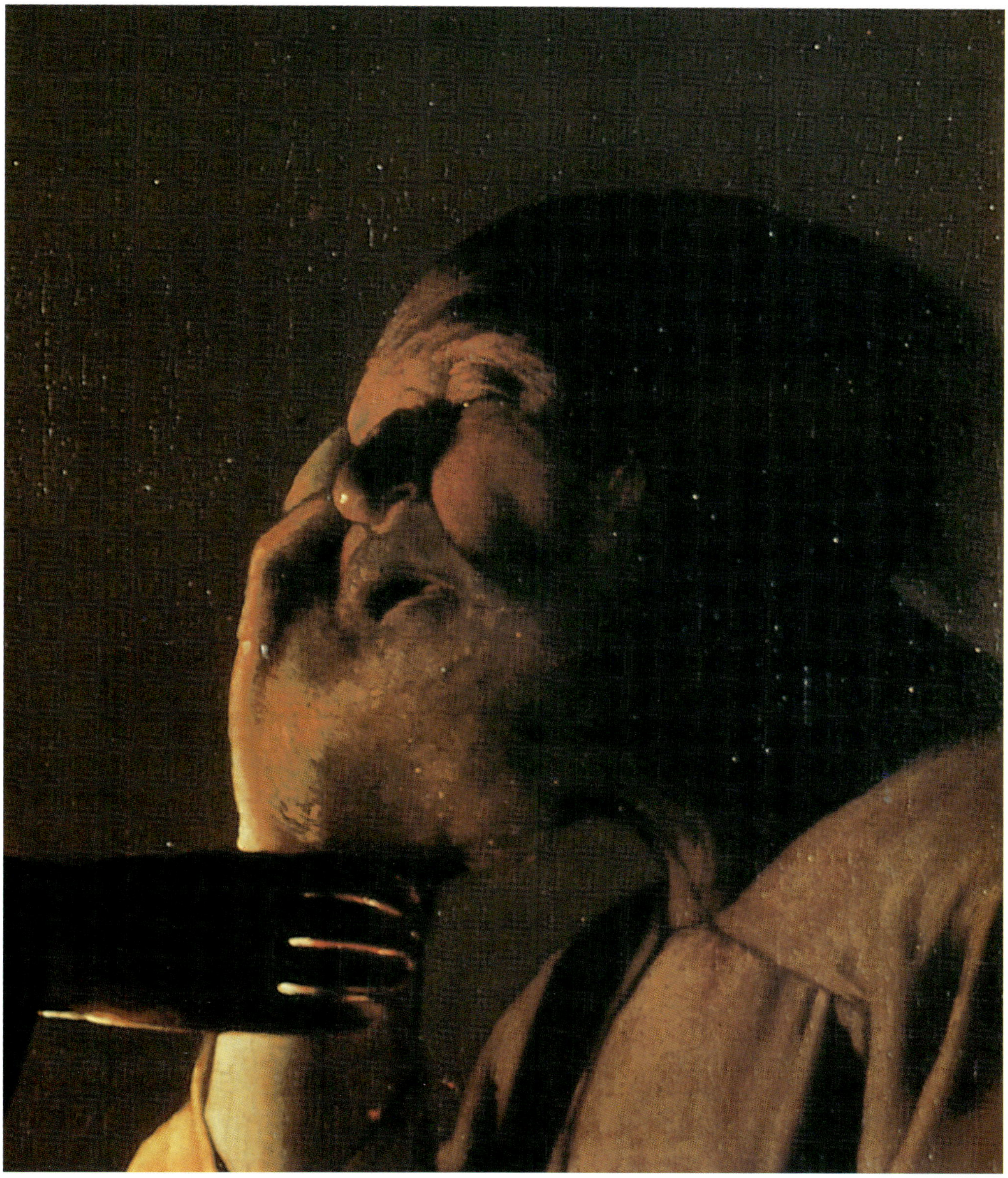

THE ANGEL APPEARS BEFORE SAINT JOSEPH.
Nantes, Musée des Beaux-Arts
detail.

"To come to the knowledge you have not,
You must go by a way in which you know not."

After he had donned the brown habit and the long white cloak of the Carmelites, he still wrote heroic verse in the pastoral style. Then he made his bed in a kneading-trough, in which he did not even put a mattress. He used a log as a pillow. In his cell in the San Andrés college, for a whole season the brothers saw him sleep like Saint Alexis on a plank under the stairs, wearing only a pair of underpants made of the esparto grass that is used to cover hen houses, whose knots were full of blood.

He had made a cross in his cell from two oak branches and a death's-head. It was in the dungeon in the prison in Toledo that he wrote the four great books that we still have by him: *The Ascent of Mount Carmel, The Dark Night of the Soul, The Spiritual Canticle* and *The Living Flame of Love,* on bits of paper brought him by Brother John of Saint Mary.

"Where are you hiding
In the dark night?
I well know the spring that flows and runs..."

The Discalced Friars used to sing the poems from *The Dark Night* during the recreation that followed the midday meal. Saint John was so absorbed in his cell that he frequently fell into an

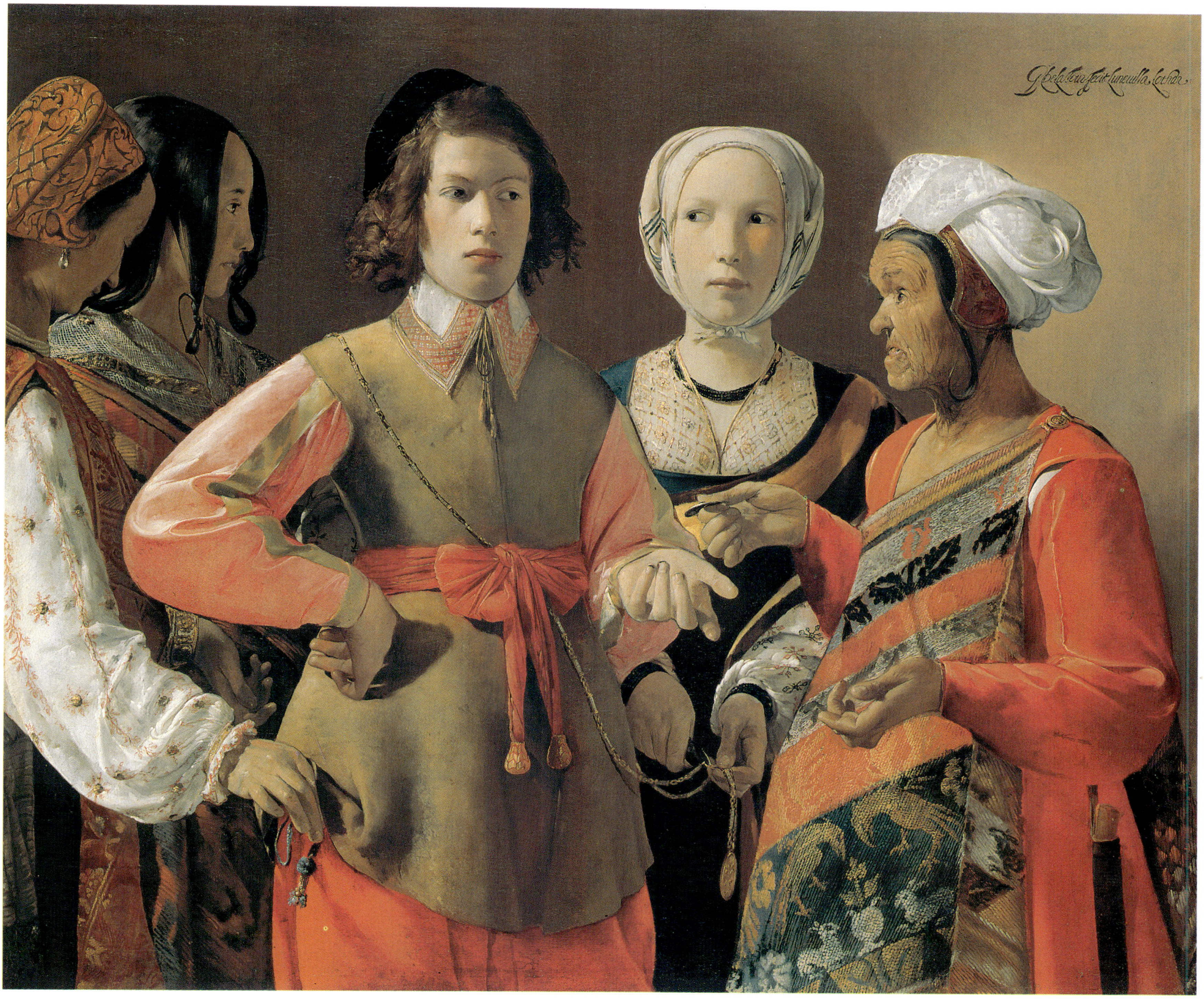

THE FORTUNETELLER.
New York, Metropolitan Museum
102 × 123 cm.

ecstatic trance, and Brother Mauricio would remain by his side until he came back to himself, because he was as bewildered as a little child when he regained consciousness. As for him, during the recreation, when he was not in a swoon, he amused himself by making little wicker baskets, or carving wooden images.

Because they are so simple, and have no names, all the canvases Georges de La Tour painted have become obscure. The painting in the museum in Mons was entitled "Monk Praying beside a Dying Monk." Then it was called "Two Monks in a cell." To me, it is the discalced saint, the prior of the Granada Carmelites, while he is with God and Brother Mauricio is watching over him.

Charles Sterling understood the painting thus: a screen masks the flame. A monk whose face is already convulsed by the other world, holding a skull in his hands, is succoured in his last hour by the prayer of a friar of his order.

Paul Jamot understood the painting thus: a screen masks the flame. Saint Francis, while meditating on death, falls into an ecstatic trance. Beatitude transfigures his face and convulses his body. A friar succours him during this loss of consciousness: he stops reading the sacred text to Francis. He raises his clasped hands as a sign of thanksgiving to God for the favour he has granted the

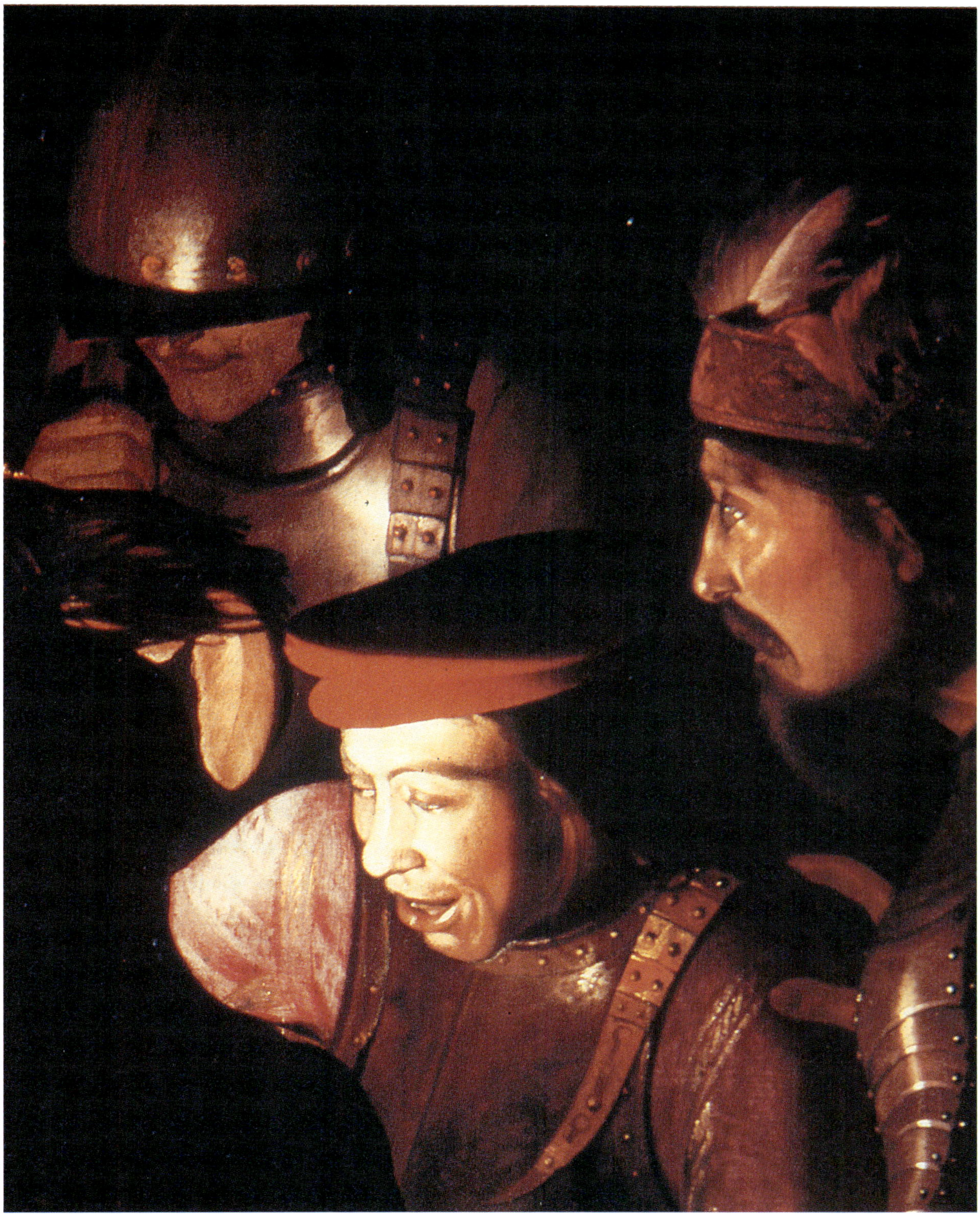

SAINT. PETER'S RENUNCIATION. 1650
Nantes, Musée des Beaux-Arts
detail.

Seraphic Father. The title could be "The Interrupted Reading."

François-Georges Pariset said that La Tour's works were anything but spontaneous. He even wrote of La Tour's "pensoir" — a place where one withdraws to think and meditate in isolation. Saint Francis's eyelids are lowered. It is the "raptus" of the saint. It is the sudden and total irruption of God. A silent image is listening to what the mystic called "the concert of angels." Through the lieutenant-general of Vic, Georges de La Tour had read the works of Saint Francis and Saint John. The title ought to be *Saint Francis in Seventh Heaven*, or *Saint John Takes Himself for a Goldfinch.*

The picture that has been called *The Dream of Saint Joseph* is even more mysterious.

There is a table between a child and an old man. There is a copper candlestick on the table. On the left, the child is standing with his left hand raised, his right arm outstretched. On the right, the old man has fallen asleep with his elbow on the table, an open book on his knees. The child is very pale, asexual, dressed in brown. The braid round his neck is pink, his waistband yellow. Looming up out of the darkness, the child may perhaps be no more than a dream. His outstretched hand doesn't yet quite touch the old man's wrist. Curiously enough, this hand does not cast a shadow on the

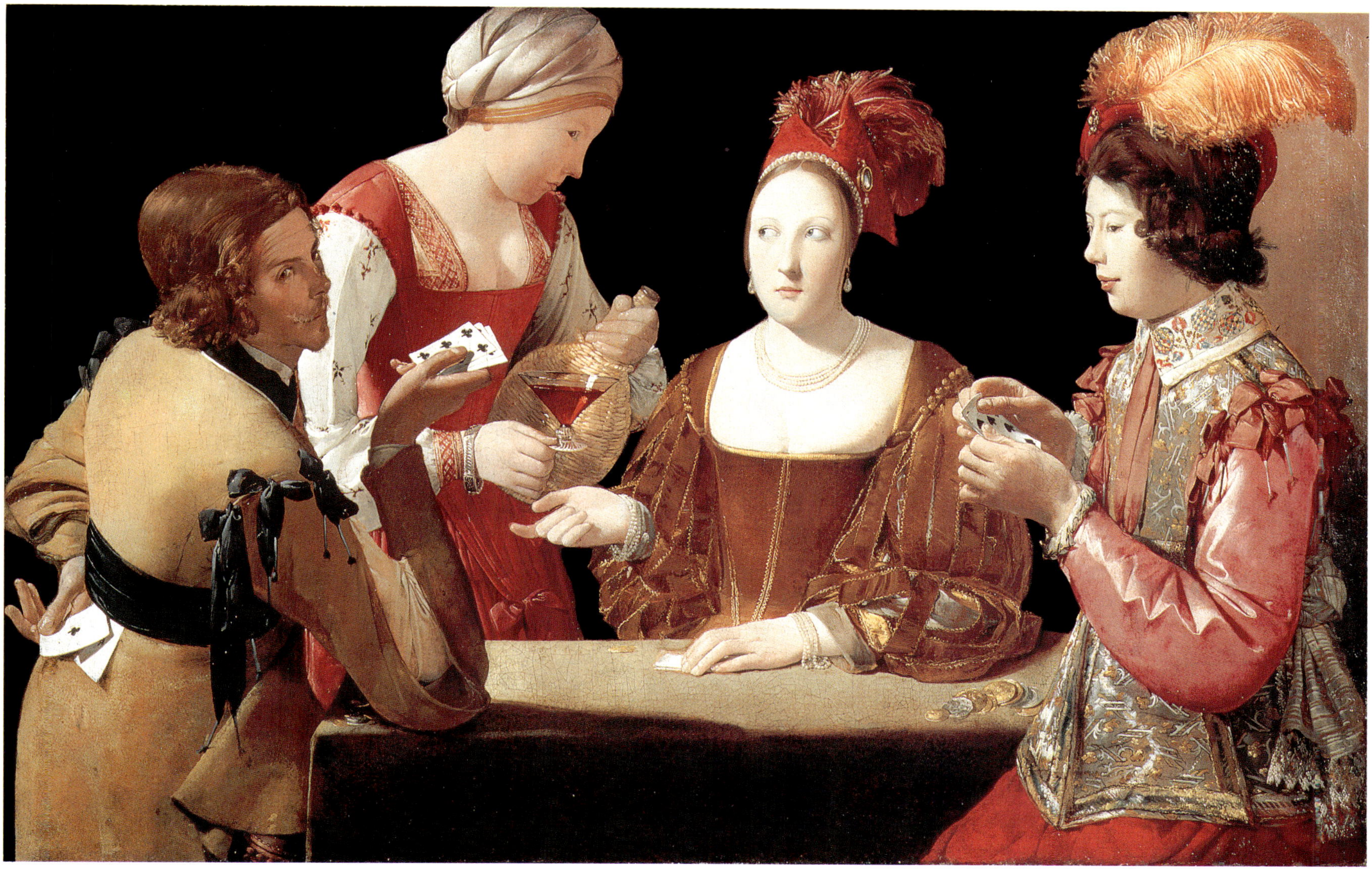

THE CHEATER
(with the ace of clubs).
Fort Worth, Kimbell Art Museum
96 × 155 cm.

sleeper's chest. Ghosts are recognisable by the inability of their vanished bodies to cast a shadow on things.

A tired man was reading, and has either given himself up to meditation, or is musing, or is in a swoon, or has fallen asleep. The ghost or the angel or the child is gazing beyond the old man. His mouth is open; perhaps he is speaking. Paul Jamot thought he was the angel liberating Saint Peter.

We must submit to our dreams, resign ourselves to discovering in them the reasons for the decisions we take. If we do not, we expose ourselves to the risk of reliving them impatiently during the day. The three night pieces that concern Joseph are to be found in Matthew. An angel in a dream orders Joseph to take Mary as his wife and to give the child she is carrying the name of Jesus. An angel in a dream orders Joseph to arise, take Jesus and his mother and flee into Egypt. An angel in a dream informs Joseph that Herod is dead, and tells him to return to the land of Israel. One of these dreams is perhaps this painting. But where is it written that Joseph read?

Or perhaps it is Matthew himself: he is listening to the angel who is murmuring to him the divine words that constitute his gospel. He has the book on his knees.

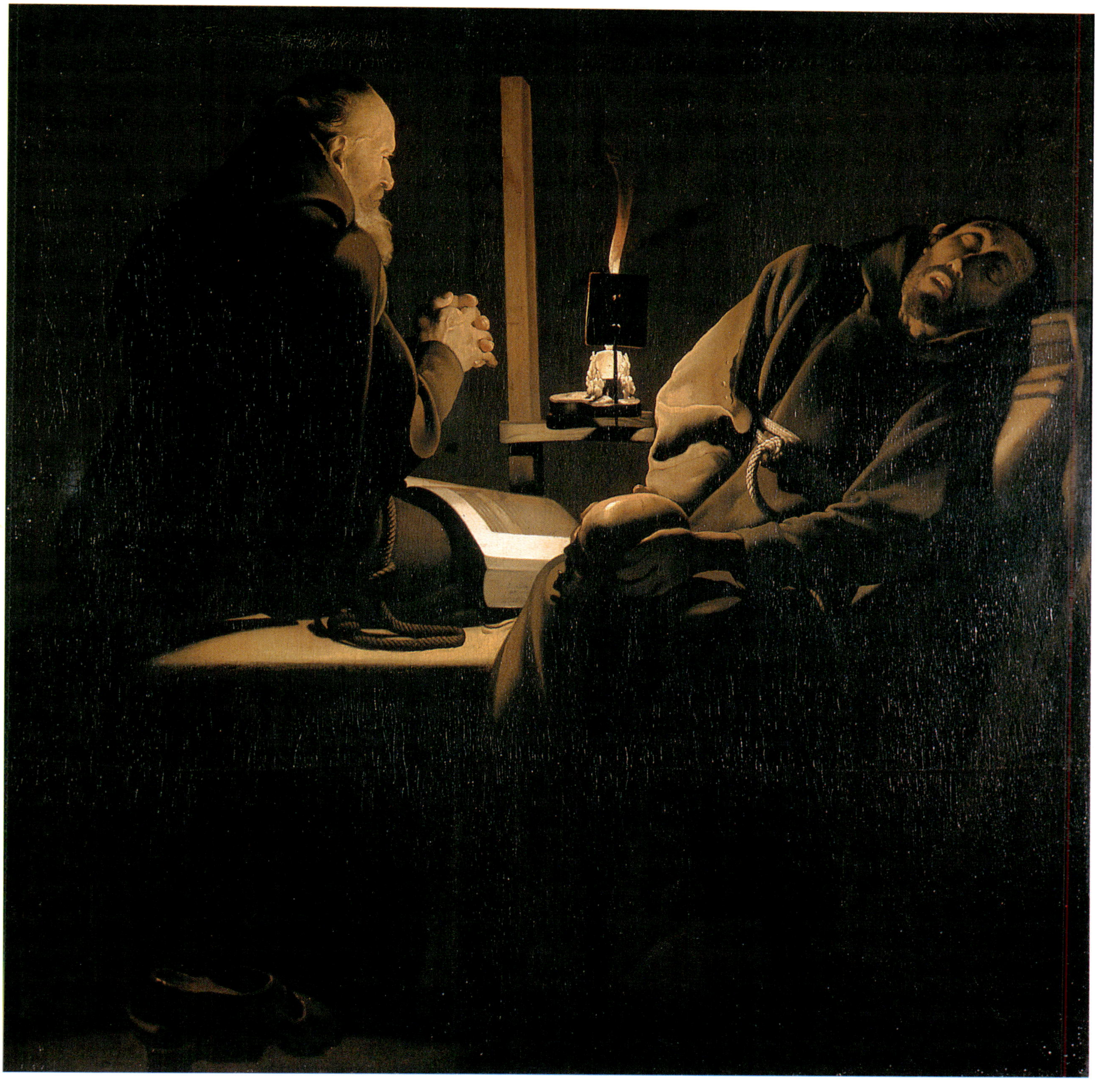

THE EXTASY OF SAINT. FRANCIS.
Le Mans, Musée Tessé
154 × 163 cm.

III

La Tour is the master of night pieces. He is the master of gazes turned inwards. He is the master with the lowered eyelids. He became rich. The Duc de la Ferté liked him: he owned six night pieces. Louis XIII admired him. Dom Calmet relates that on the day Georges de La Tour presented the king with "a painting of his own composition which represented a Saint Sebastian at night, this work was in so perfect a style that the King had all the other pictures removed from his chamber and left only that one." Le Nôtre, Rambervillers, Louvois collected him. Alphonse de Rambervillers, born in Toul in 1560, had studied in Toulouse with the brother of Louis XIII's Minister of Justice, Guillaume du Vair. De Rambervillers was the lieutenant-general of the bailiwick of Vic. He was a Renaissance man, a classical scholar, an antiquary, a collector. He built up one of the most valuable collections in Lorraine. More than anything in the world, in poetry, he loved stanzas; in painting, night pieces; and in stones, antique enamels. He used to exchange pieces with Nicolas de Peiresc. Through Sébastien Cramoisy, Peiresc bought works by Jacques Callot. Alphonse de Rambervillers said that he had "a natural proclivity

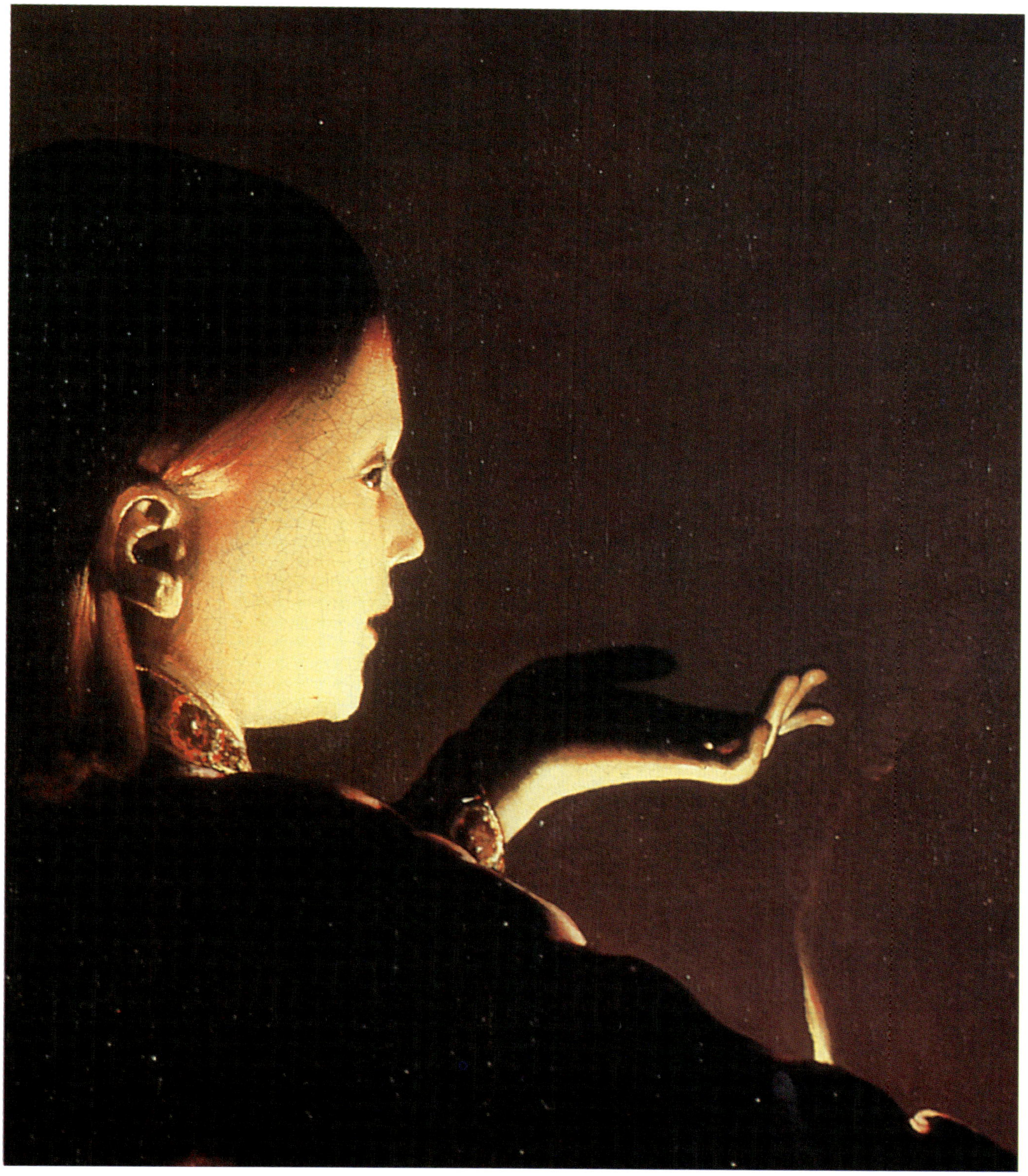

THE ANGEL APPEARS BEFORE SAINT. JOSEPH.
Nantes, Musée des Beaux-Arts
detail.

towards painting," and preferred to buy La Tours. As Louis XIII had not granted him the recompense that Henri IV had contracted to give him, for the rest of his life de Rambervillers wrote long complaints about kings' unkept promises. "I shall retire into myself, deploring the condition of lettered men who plough a totally sterile field." This letter is dated March 27, 1621, from Vic. He wrote devotional books, at the same time as stanzas. In his *Saint Livier* he writes of "the lamentable face of all things" revealed by the flames and the feeling of desolation caused by outbreaks of fire. The word "lamentable" is to be taken in the sense of the prophet Jeremiah and of the *Lamentations* at the Tenebrae service. He adds: "being very certain that nothing is so affecting as domestic examples." Monsieur de Rambervillers became a cousin by marriage of Georges de La Tour: on July 2, 1617, he was a witness at his marriage to Diane Le Nerf. La Tour's painting is dedicated to this "lamentable face" of things in their domestic nudity.

He was rich and famous. The Capuchins bought him. The Minims and Saint John of the Cross's Carmelites overran Metz, Rennes, Vic, Lunéville, and coveted his canvases. In Lunéville, he was almost a nobleman. When he was fifty-two he kept a pack of hounds and went hunting. In 1646, the

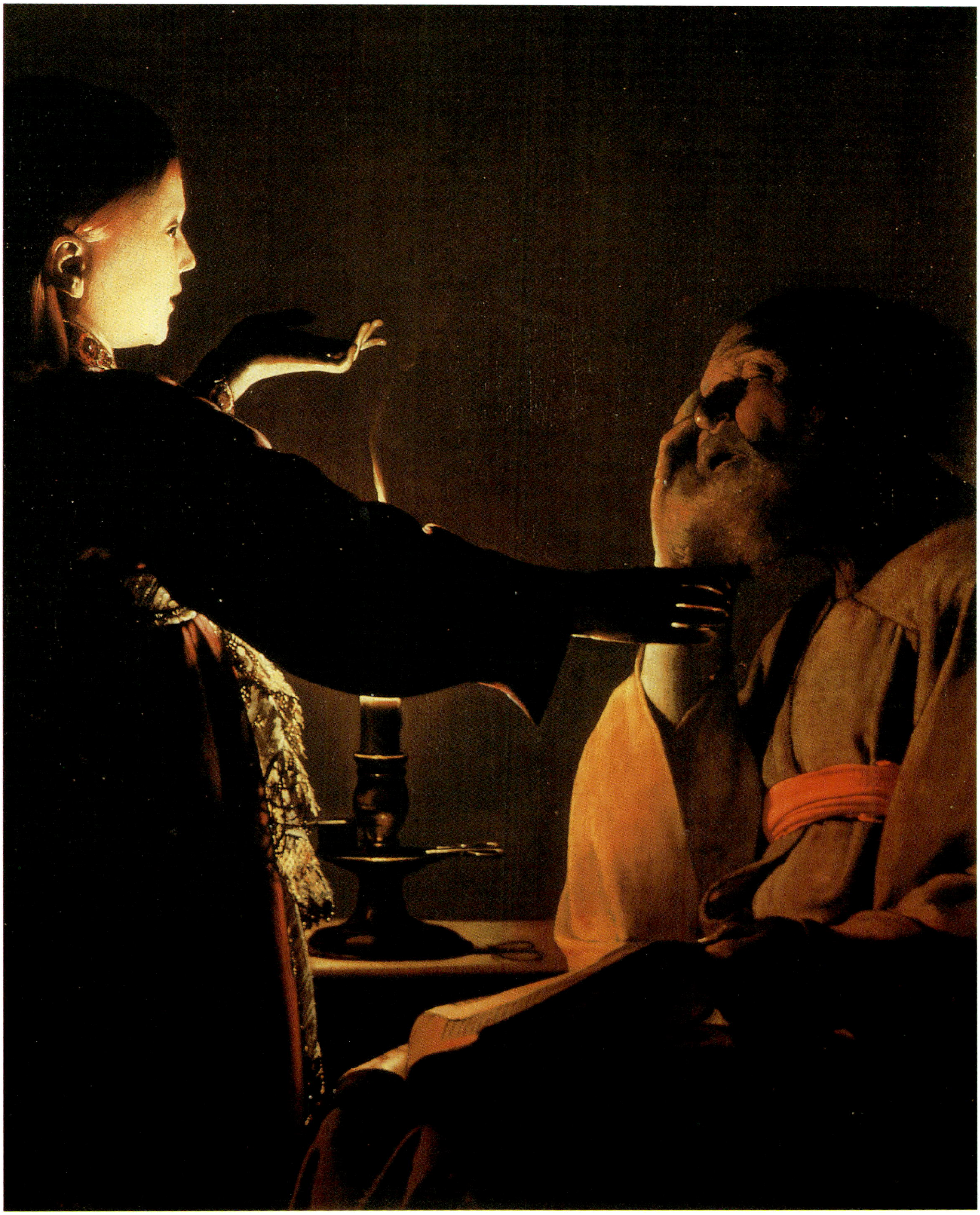

THE ANGEL APPEARS BEFORE SAINT.JOSEPH
Nantes, Musée des Beaux-Arts
93 × 81 cm.

inhabitants of Lunéville addressed a petition to the Duke of Lorraine complaining about the painter who owned "a third of all the livestock in Lunéville. Monsieur Georges La Tour, painter, is making himself obnoxious to everyone by the great number of dogs, greyhounds and spaniels he keeps, acting as though he were the Lord of the Manor, sending his dogs after hare into the standing crops, which they trample down and ruin."

Saint Joseph is in his carpenter's shop: it is a stifling cellar. This is La Tour's first great monochrome. The two figures are not aware that they are seen. Georges de la Tour always succeeds in giving this impression of distance and eternal immobility. Saint Joseph is thin, and the hollows in his body are painted with such realism as to suggest that the hunger he has formerly known still torments him. The child bringing the light is an apparition wearing monks' pattens, his knees are strongly lit, his tunic is tied very high up. The hand holding the candle is the only one to have such long fingers. His face is the real focal point of the light, full lips, his eye wide open on to greater and more distant things than those he sees.

The man is strength itself become flesh, a big apron tied at the waist, swollen veins on his forehead, muscles that stand out, enormous hands, wide feet. The child's gaze is very tender, fearless,

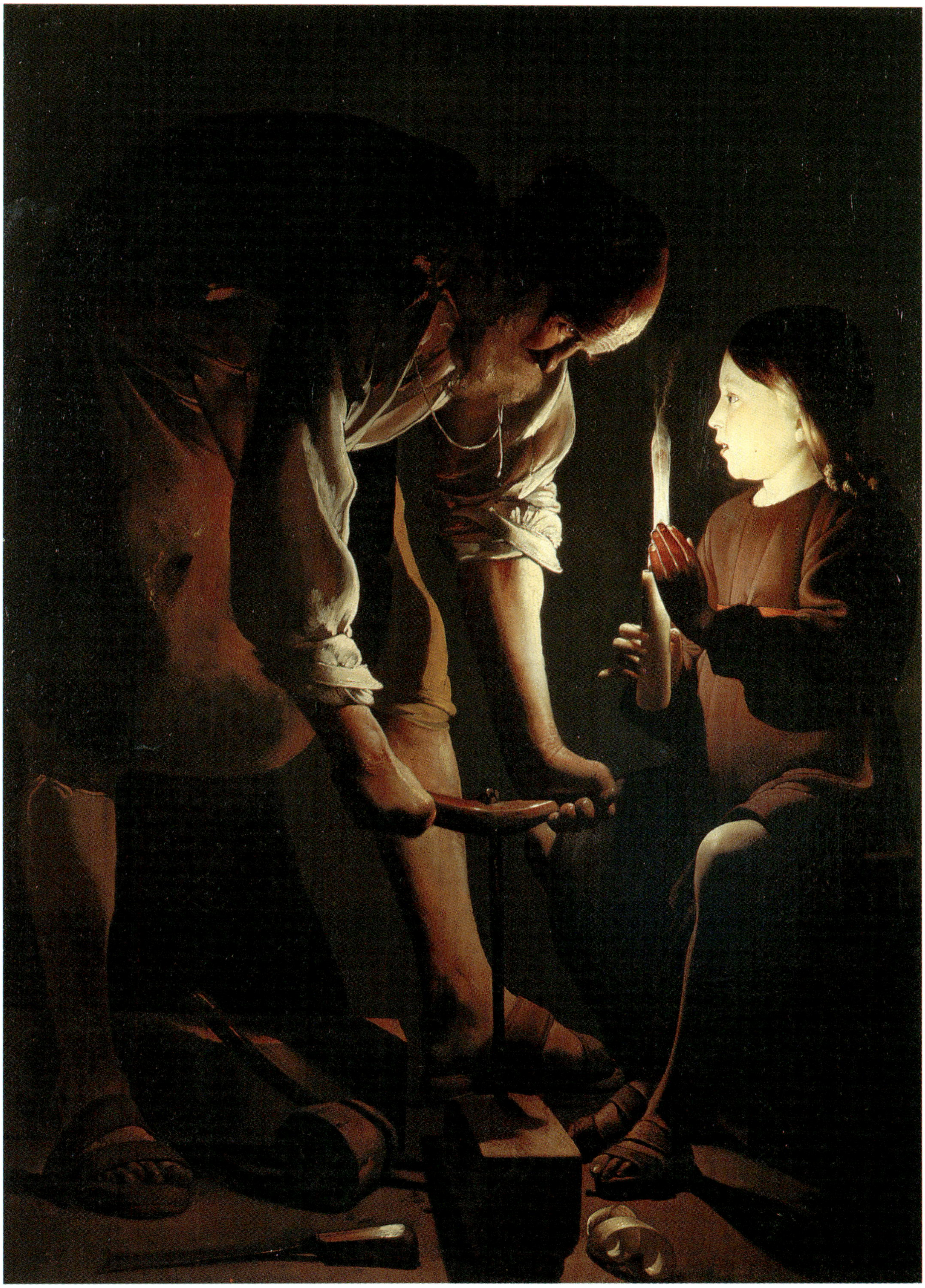

SAINT. JOSEPH THE CARPENTER.
Paris, Musée du Louvre
137 × 101 cm.

and he is contemplating. The brown and blue objects are seen from above: two wooden blocks, a mallet, an auger, a chisel. Aided by the auger and the muscles, the cross begins to rise in the image. And then we realise the object of the young god's melancholy dream. He feels divinity growing in him as the cross grows under his father's fingers. This scene might be called: *The Cross Grows.* There is a life hidden in childhood which is the prefiguration of what is going to be lived, and which permeates it. A carpenter's son can only end by being nailed on to wood. A baker's son can only end in the carmine images cooking in the oven during the last hours of the night. The child still retains the secret of the kingdom of non-language, in the same way as the short period of childhood establishes the enigma that only the future and the last breath reveal.

IV

Gonse's comment when he rediscovered La Tour in 1900 is famous: "Like good old La Fontaine who asked everyone he met: have you read

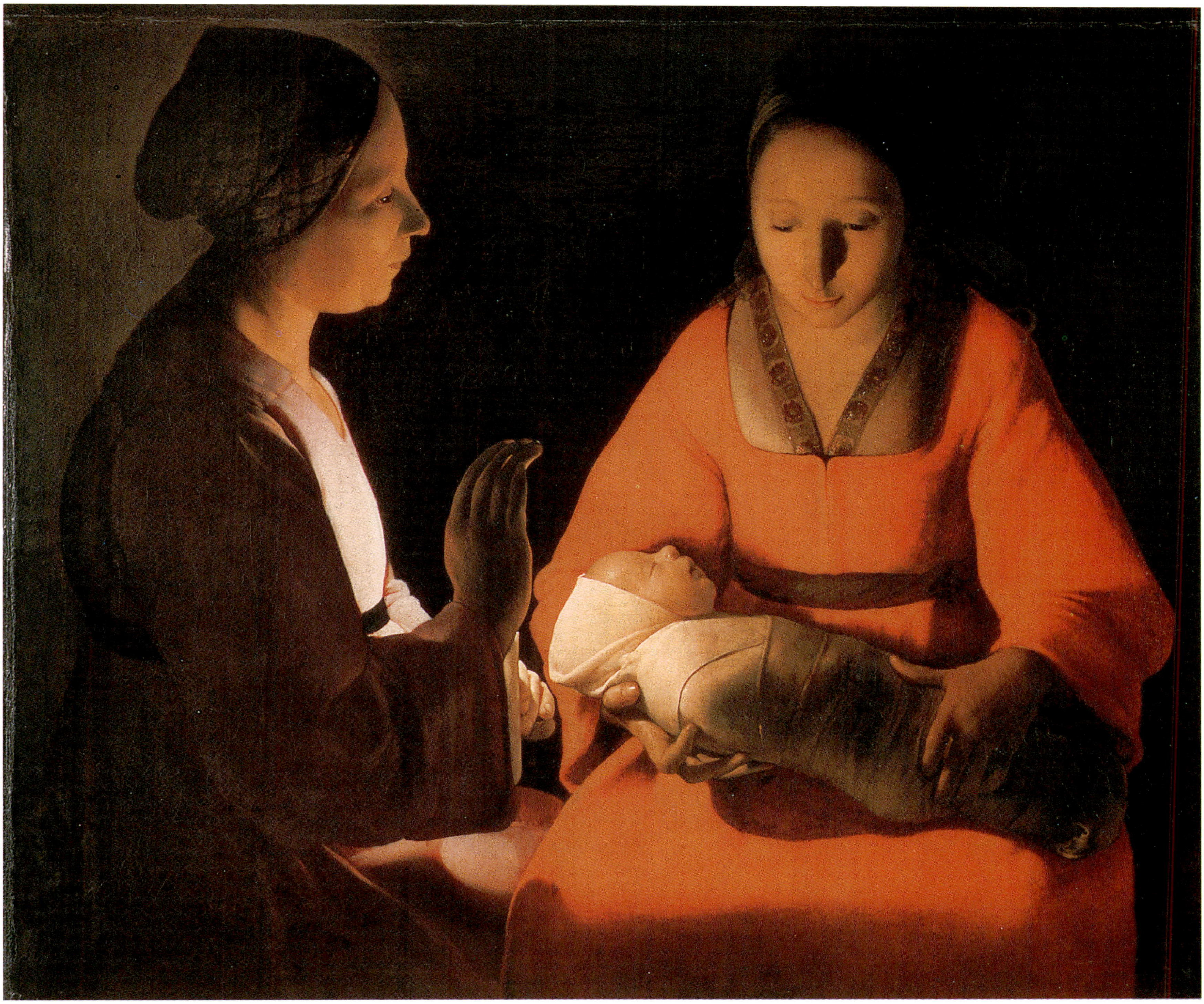

THE NEWBORN.
Rennes, Musée des Beaux-Arts
76 × 91.

Baruch? I would like to keep shouting to the four winds: do you know that delightfully strange painting of a newborn child in the Rennes museum?" In *The Newborn Child,* the candlelight is masked behind the raised hand. The hand hesitates between blessing or protecting the flame, and is concentrated on the enigma of a tiny little man bound in swaddling clothes, who will one day be dead. The baby becomes the focal point whose light carves solicitude on the faces of the two young women bending over him. In La Tour, gods have no haloes, angels have no wings, and ghosts have no shadows. We do not know whether it is a child or Jesus. Or rather: every child is Jesus. Every woman bending over her newborn baby is Mary watching over a son who is going to die. La Tour does not paint pictures, but images. In Rome, they gave the name of image to the wax death masks that were worn at funerals and stored in a little cupboard in the atrium. Only nobles had a right to these images. The ancestors are the household gods. In our nightmares, death masks become gods.

The paintings do not tell a story, they create a silence, while remaining on the watch for the story. They transform life into its résumé. They turn mystery into everything that is most domestic, while at the same time suddenly solemnising the

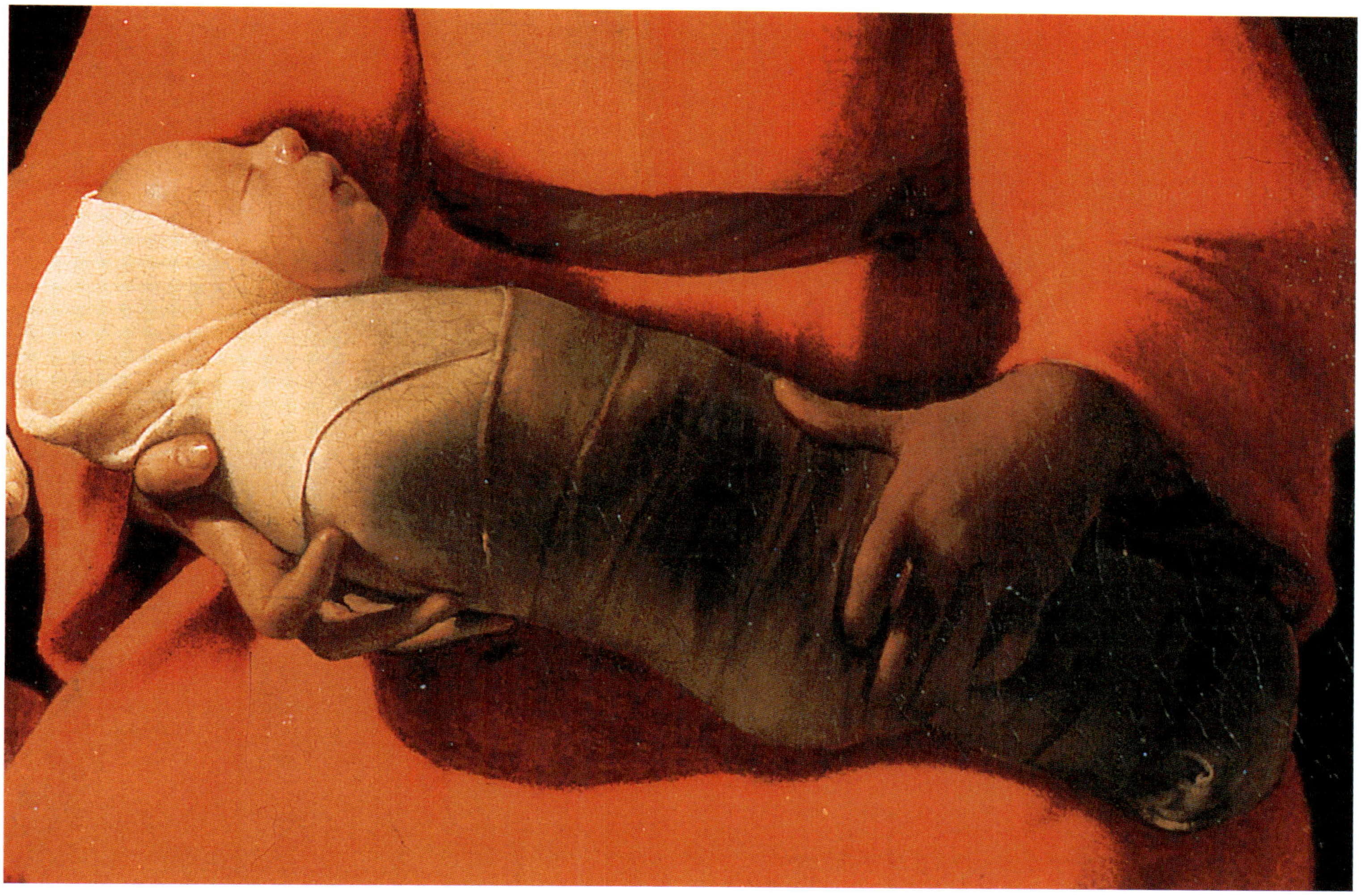

THE NEWBORN.
Rennes, Musée des Beaux-Arts
detail.

molecules of the human condition: birth, separation, sexuality, abandonment, silence, agony, death.

Jacques Esprit spoke of the "economical ostentation" of humility. One could speak of the sanctity of ordinary things. The devotion to Saint Joseph, which increased throughout the seventeenth century, plunged the divine mystery into the most ordinary, day-to-day appearance. John of the Cross had made Joseph the saint of the Discalced Friars. The gleam, the silence, and the darkness consecrate every ordinary individual and turn him into an ageless hero of legend. They amplify, by simplicity and nocturnal monochromy. The more this amplitude is simplified, the more monumental it becomes; and the more obscure it is, the more simplified.

Everything is unique, and everything is double. Every woman is Mary — but everyone dies. It is never the same happiness that is shattered when a man and a woman become estranged, even if it is always an eternally similar embrace that unites a man and a woman when they love one another. It is never the same tear that flows, even if it is always the same desertion that causes the same suffering. It is never just any man who dies, even if it has always been the same death that deprives our breathing of air and our vision of light. *The*

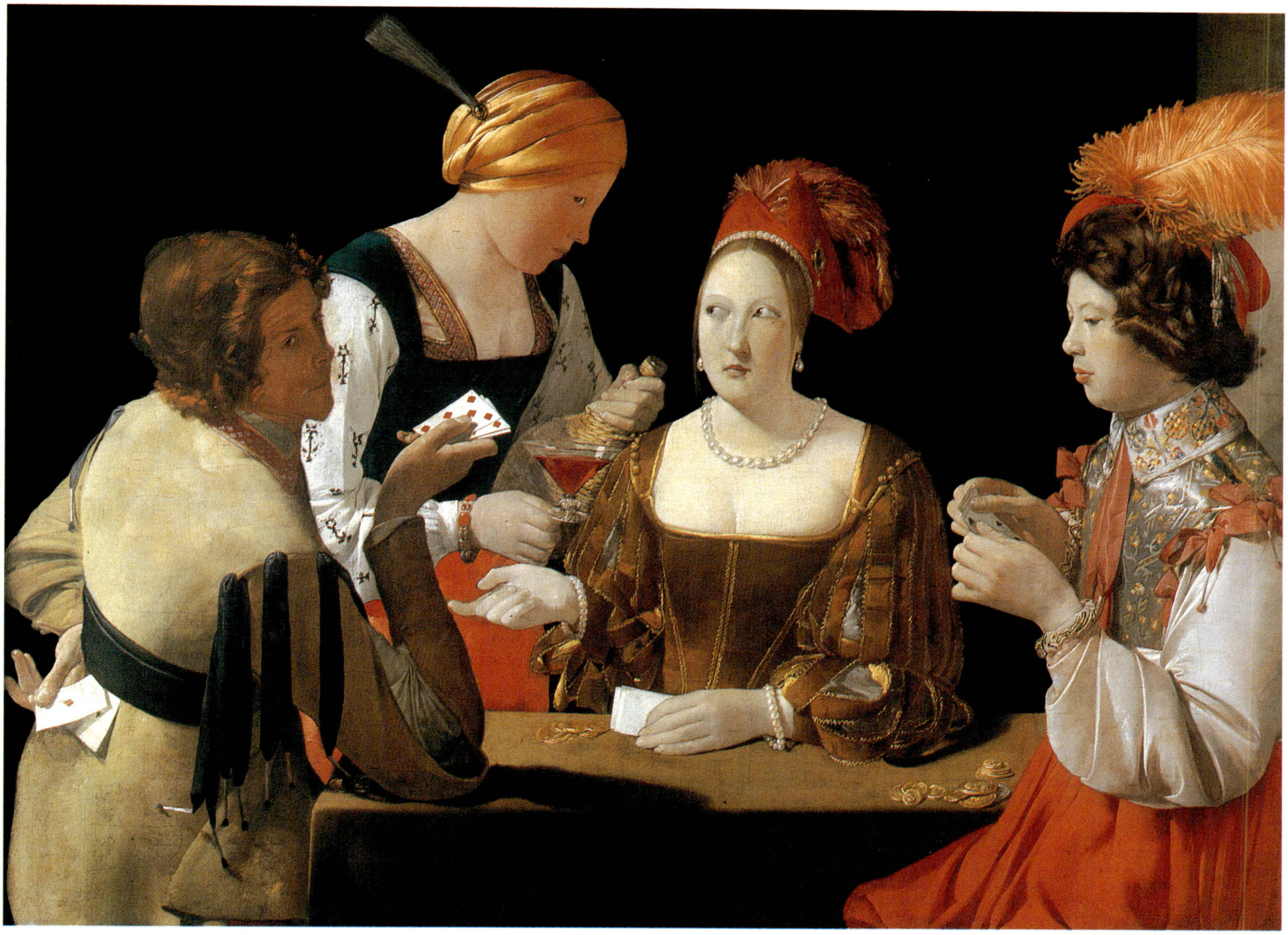

THE CHEATER
(with the ace of diamonds).
Paris, Musée du Louvre
106 × 146 cm.

Newborn Child is the opposite of an *Adoration.* In 1640, in Paris, the Reverend Capuchin Father Sébastien de Senlis published a book entitled *The Torch of the Just.* On page 272 of the first volume he noted: "If you look at those little Babes in the arms of their Nurses, swathed in their little Swaddling Clothes, would not the sight of them cause you to say that they are Prisoners, pinioned thus for very great crimes? They are nevertheless young Slaves whom the sins of their Fathers keep confined in Shackles." Anne, if it is Anne, is in profile. Mary, if it is Mary, is full face. The down on the baby's face near his bonnet is reddish. He has no eyebrows, his eyes are closed, his nose retroussé, his big lips half open for his breath or for air. The old title was *The Watching Women,* or *The Dead Child.* We don't know whether he is a dead child or a little god. If it is Anne, there is a bitter twist to her lips. She is anticipating the tragic destiny. The mother, with lowered eyes, is not looking at the child but contemplating something that is more distant than the body she is holding. If it is Mary, she is contemplating the distant Passion. Extraordinarily, her lips seem to be smiling with suffering, youth, sadness, pride.

The bound newborn baby is like a loaf of bread made of light. A child, in 1660, watches at a distance from the narrow embrasure of the oven and

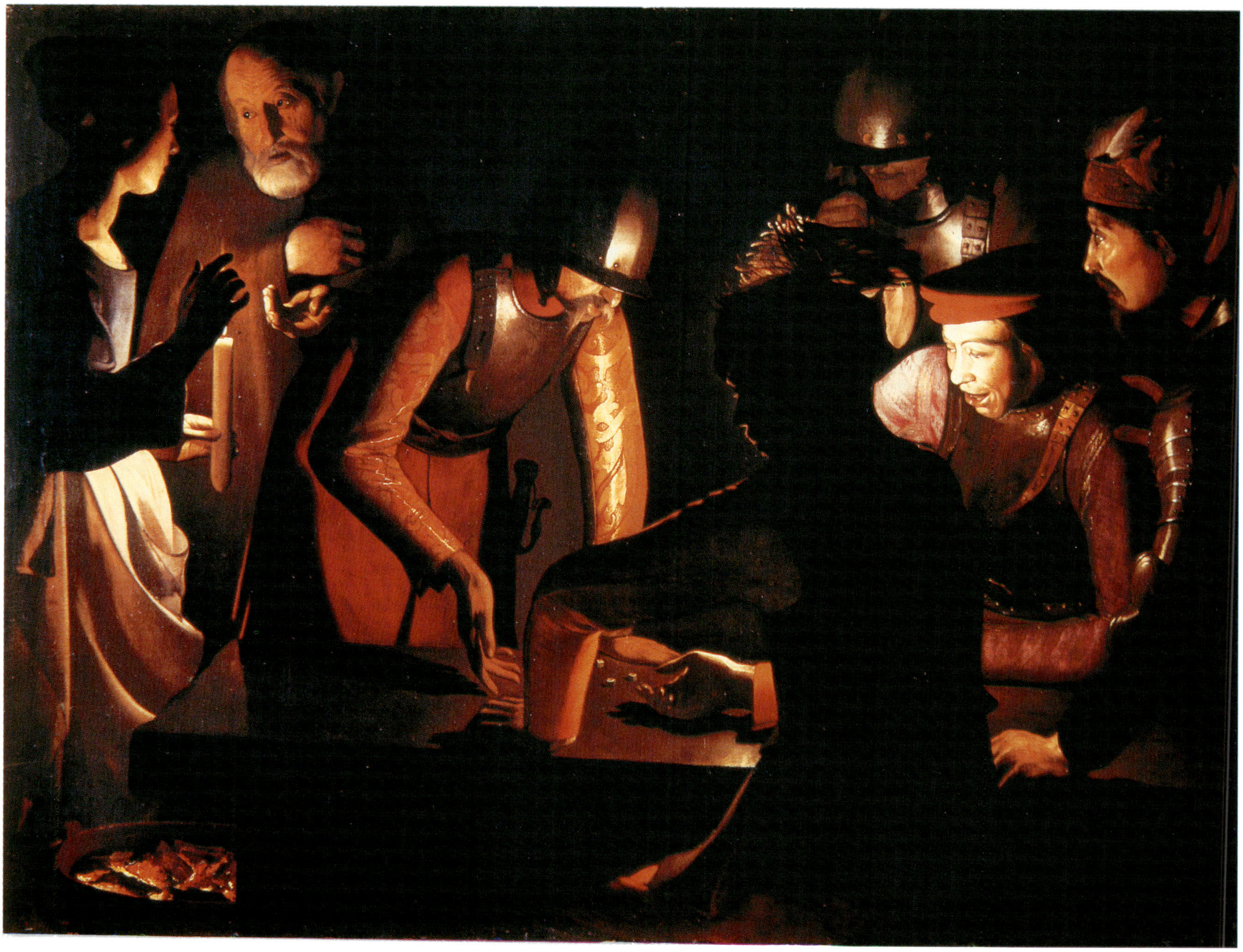

SAINT. PETER'S RENUNCIATION. 1650
Nantes, Musée des Beaux-Arts
120 × 160 cm.

waits for the bread to rise in the almost white heat, and to change colour. The event that led Georges de La Tour to specialise in night pieces seems to have coincided with the conflagration in Lunéville. This was during the Thirty Years' War, Lorraine was ravaged by the French troops, its castles on fire, its churches flouted, its monasteries pillaged, its pictures burned. La Tour's studio and its daylight paintings perished in the flames. This was testified to in September 1638: "When both the town and the castle were set on fire on such a dark night, it was possible to read in the glow of the fire on the little hill leading up from Lunéville to Einville." It was possible to read in the glow of the fire lit by the French. The people's distress was indescribable. Brambles and animals overran the villages, which were abandoned. Dogs and wolves dug up the dead. Jean de Ligniville counted the cases of cannibalism. Perhaps the tragic conflagration in Lunéville took the place of the nourishing fire of childhood. It is not known what La Tour did, or where he went. The town was decimated by the plague. But it is known that in his house in Lunéville, a manservant and one of of his apprentices died of the plague.

The 1646 petition against him shows him to be a man as violent as he was proud. Without charity. In 1648, he had a fight with an officer of the

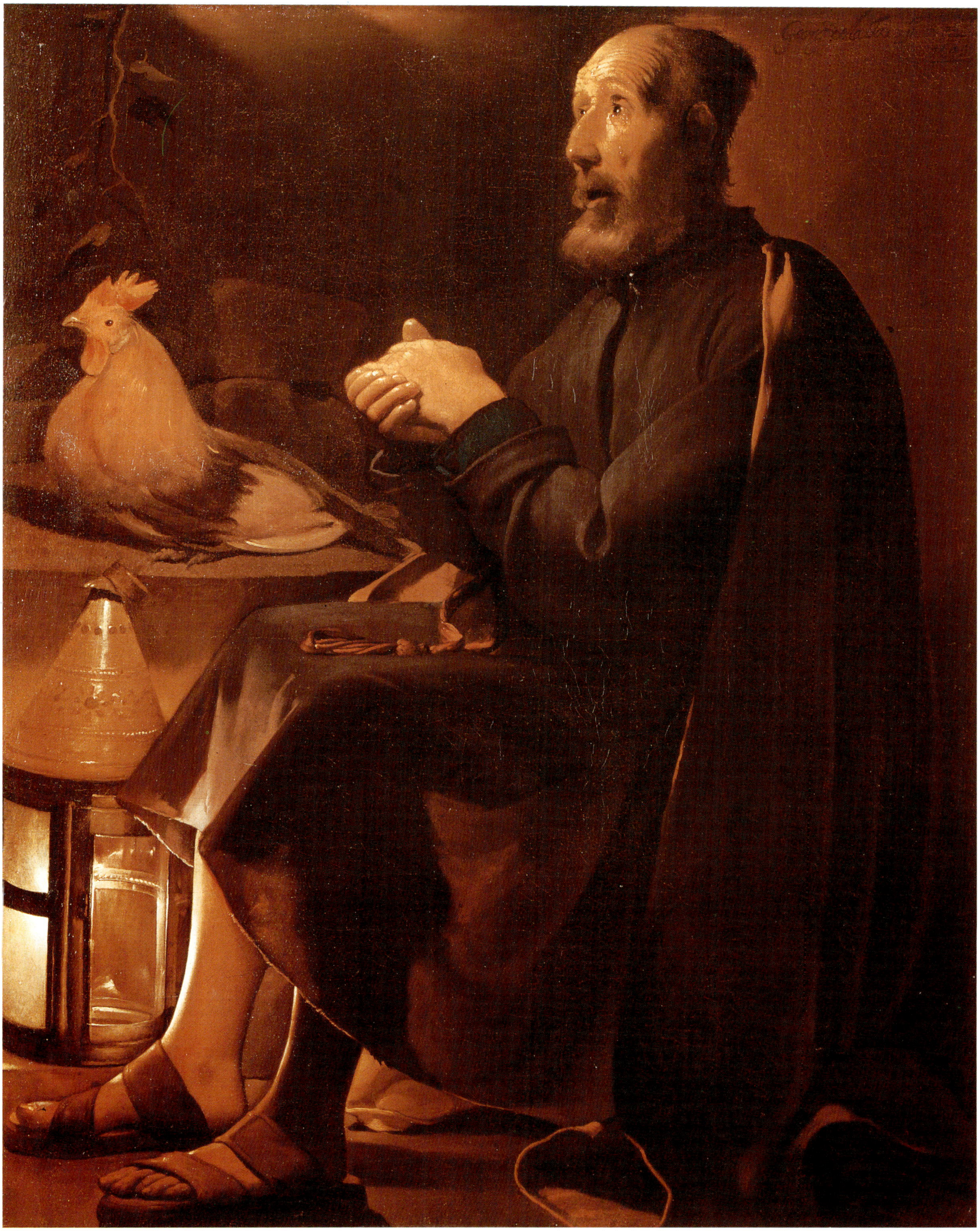

SAINT. PETER'S TEARS.
Cleveland, Museum of Art
114×95 cm.

law. Then he struck a peasant, Fleurent Louys, with a stick, and left him in a dreadful state. Here, we must once again quote Jacques Esprit : "If we had a true Idea of the Condition of Man, and if we knew that he is possessed with a Self-Love altogether violent and erroneous, and that this Self-Love renders him impetuous, wild and inhuman, the knowledge of this would spare us the trouble of shewing that Mildness is no real Vertue." Every creator is violent. Both Bach and Rameau, a hundred years later, had themselves forbidden to wear swords because they feared the desire to kill that suddenly came over them.

In 1648, La Tour's daughter Marie died. Out of ten children, he had only two daughters and a son left, Christine, Claude and Etienne. There is Mary's double. There is Mary's ghost. Which Mary is this? Stories, theologians and fairies say that we recognise the dead who return to haunt the world by their absence of colours and reflections, by the fact that they leave no shadows on walls or sandy paths.

In *The Gamblers,* the lighting is not as diurnal as has been claimed: the source of light is on the top left, outside, but extremely close and intense. It is a kind of violent neon. It isn't daylight. It's a violent light. Like the blows he deals with a stick.

In Epinal there is an image which is itself ob-

SAINT. PETER'S TEARS.
Cleveland, Museum of Art
detail.

scure and which is called *Job,* or *Job Mocked by His Wife.* This title is far from being certain. It must no doubt refer to another scene. Job of Uz was a happy, God-fearing man. The Devil tempted the Eternal. "If this man who loves you were to suffer," the Devil said to God, "he would worship you in a more disinterested fashion." So Jehovah delivered Job up to Satan. His flocks and herds perished, his children died, his fortune melted as the wax that touches the wick: Job suffered everything patiently. His wife could not bear him to bear everything with such patience, and mocked him day and night. She told him: "Stop suffering! Curse God, and die!"

Every woman is Mary. Every woman is Job's wife. She is an immense, stooping figure, engulfed in darkness like a hallucination. She is a siren, or a Theban sphinx. She is like Philosophia standing in a dream above Boethius's bed, consoling him after having terrified him. She is wearing a red dress, an écru apron, starched but barely ironed, white wristbands, a white turban. The width of the costume, the head coming into contact with the edge of the canvas and bending down, gives this body a "too big," almost superhuman quality. Her nostrils are pinched, her mouth disdainful, the fingers of her outstretched hand keep opening and closing in remonstrance. Their gazes confront one

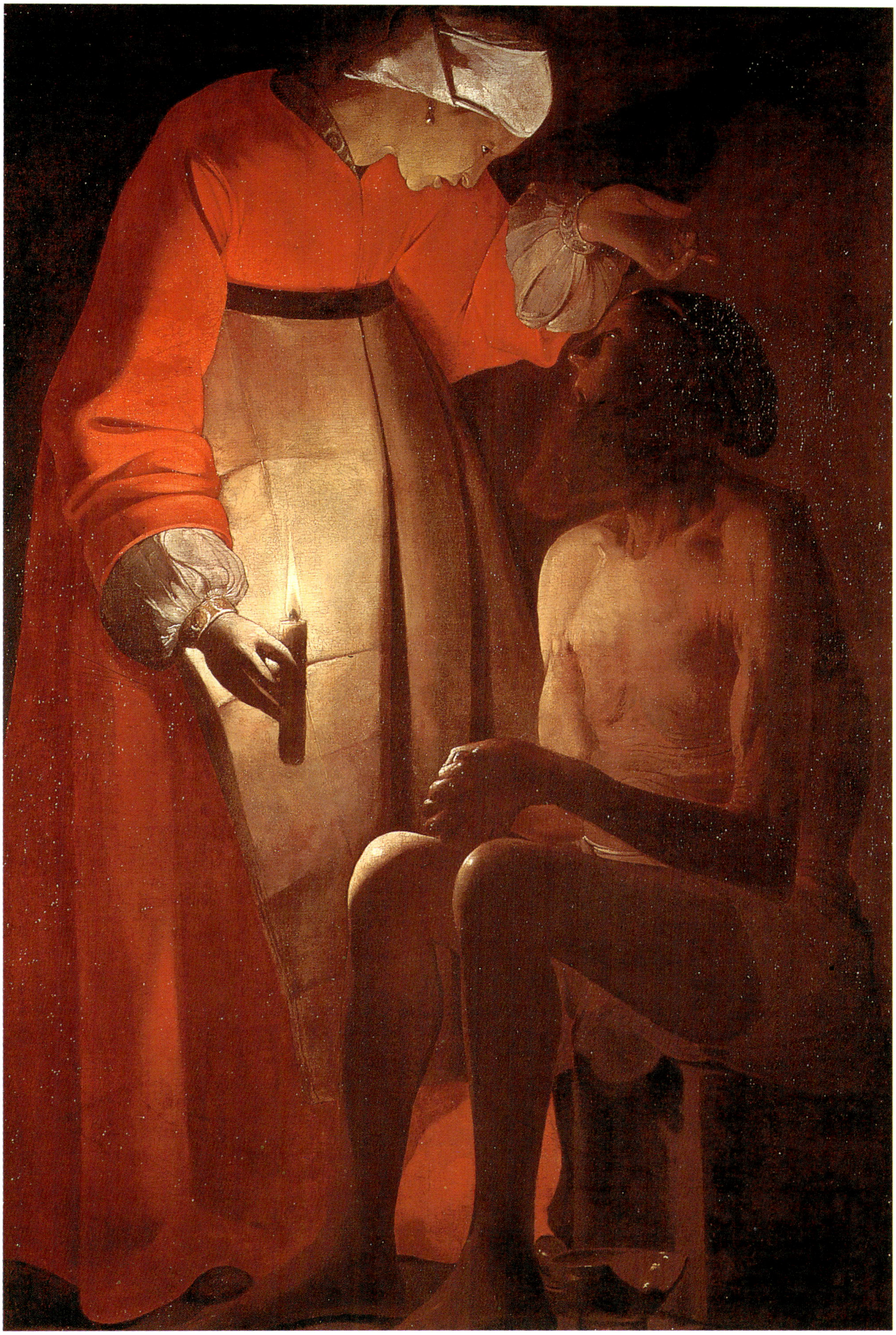

JOB AND HIS WIFE.
Epinal, Musée Départemental des Vosges
145 × 97 cm.

another. It is an interminable conflict: a dominating goddess and a sick, humiliated man.

V

This title is not certain: *The Flea.* A half-naked woman is crushing a flea between her fingers. It is the world she is crushing. I think Georges de La Tour, like the faithful who went to the Tenebrae service in Holy Week to hear Jeremiah's *Lamentations* and the destructive vocalises, was thinking of the prophet Jeremiah's verse: "I beheld the earth, and lo, it was without form, and void."

This painting has always been considered profane. It has been given three meanings: the pains of childbirth, the repentant servant, a woman crushing a louse or a flea between her two nails. A man paints his fellow human beings. With the confidence of a child, he questions what is in front of his eyes. This confidence that children have is also dismay. He is fascinated by the humanity of man; by the body that incarnates him; by the fear that paralyses him; by the death that he fears; by the gleam that illuminates him. In the seventeenth

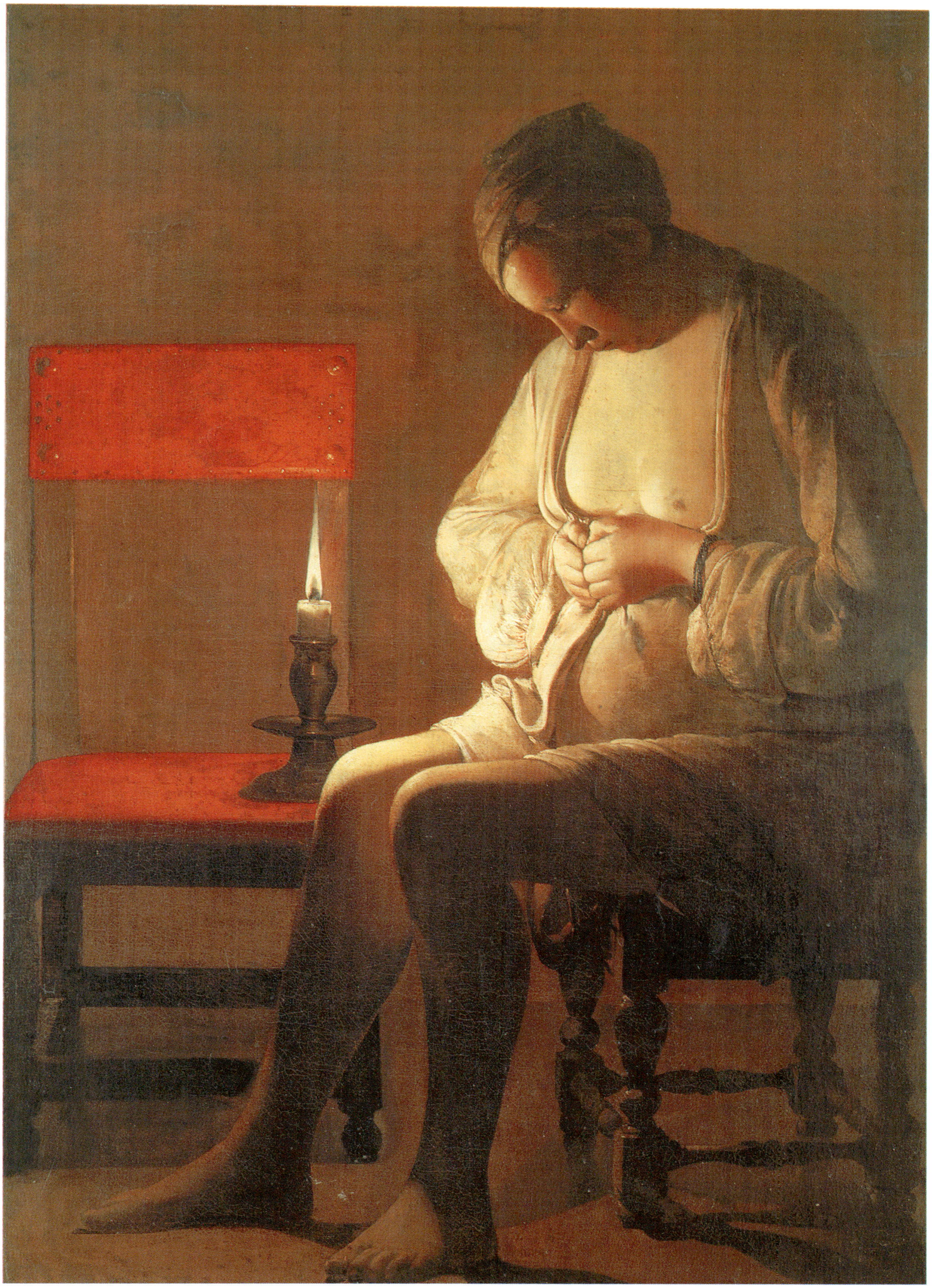

THE WOMAN AND THE FLEA.
Nancy, Musée Historique Lorrain
120 × 90 cm.

century they gave the name of "silent paintings" to what we call "still lifes." These are silent paintings: like a moth or a beetle scorching its wings in a candle, this is a woman disinfesting herself. In the silence, we can hear the sputtering sound of the silence; the person watching becomes inexplicably attentive; and a prayer is sent up.

Tension — that is the baroque, as it is also the form of the enigma. The simplicity of the make-up of a page, the clarity of drawing of forms, the simplicity of tones — all these seem classic, but the antithesis that underlies them and the unreality resulting from this realism carried to the extreme of starkness, are anything but classic. Pascal juxtaposes opposites with fanatical passion. La Tour immobilises them in a glowing calm, a speaking silence. In canvas after canvas, as in Jacques Esprit's *The Falsity of Human Virtues,* the worldly interests and concupiscences that torment men's principles are laid bare, and make an oblation to the other world.

He did not paint landscapes, skyscapes, water, clouds. One does not need to be God in order to be great. One does not need gold, beauty, ornament, in order to be loved: the slightest desire against the background of death is enough.

The background of Georges de La Tour's paintings is not black, or brown, or pearl grey, it is:

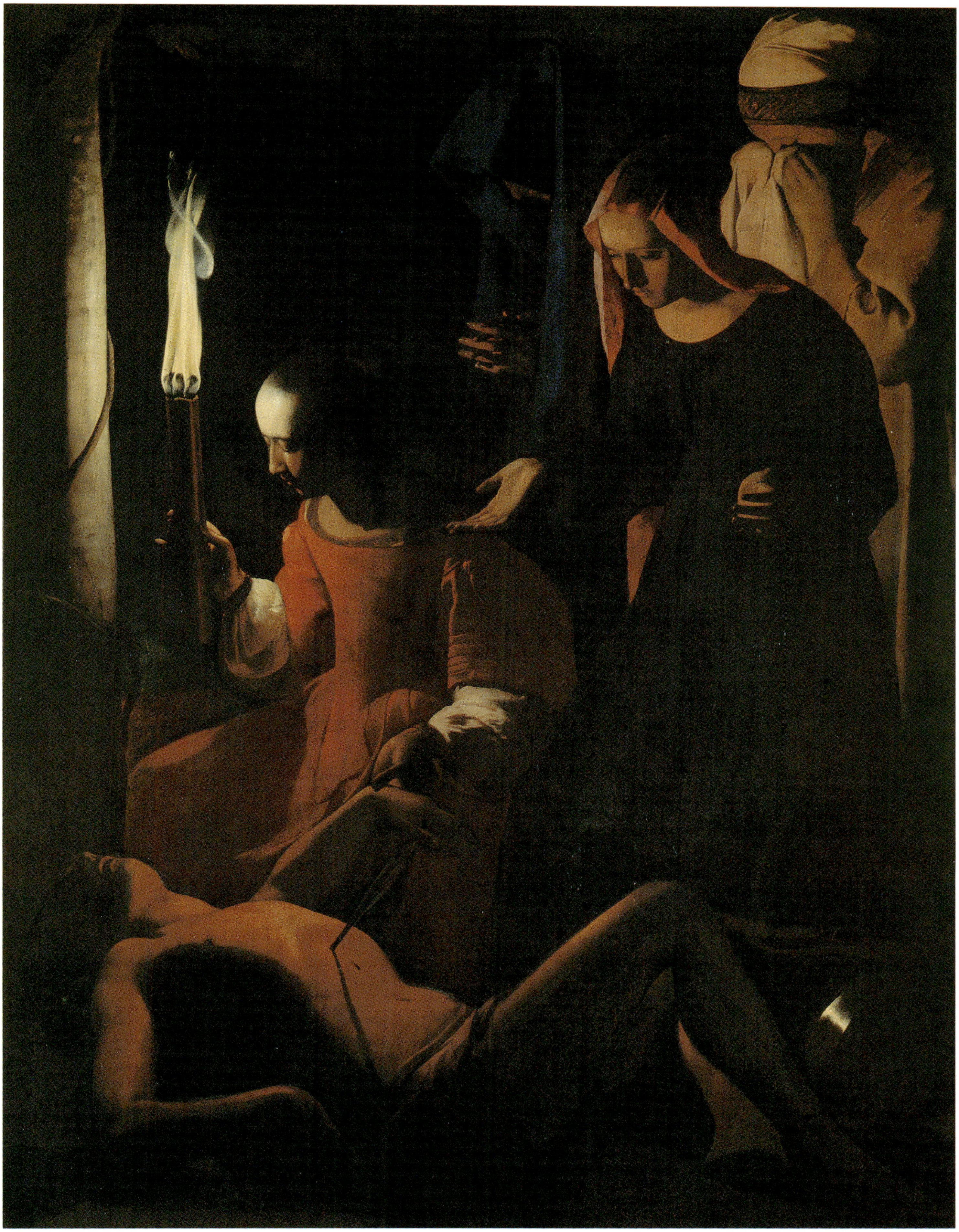

IRENE TENDING TO SAINT. SEBASTIAN
(with torch).
Paris, Musée du Louvre
167 × 130 cm.

"We die."

I shall never be able to understand why this woman is so very unerotic, when after all she is so feminine, and young, and beautiful. This scene, which is so extremely intimate and so extremely lowly — almost like one of the chimpanzees or marmosets in a zoo — could have been taken up by Fragonard. It is as far as possible removed from Fragonard. An incomprehensible pity and gravity emanates from the flea or louse remover. Whatever its cause, this nudity is religious. Reading, praying, listening to a Tenebrae lesson, contemplating a night piece, are one single spiritual exercise. This painting, whose subject we know nothing of, preserves its enigma.

VI

At the beginning of 1652, on January 15, his wife died. On the 22nd, his manservant died. On the 30th, he died.

Euphormion was the richest citizen in Rome, and he was a prefect. He was married to Aglaia. They had a son, whom they called Alexis. On his

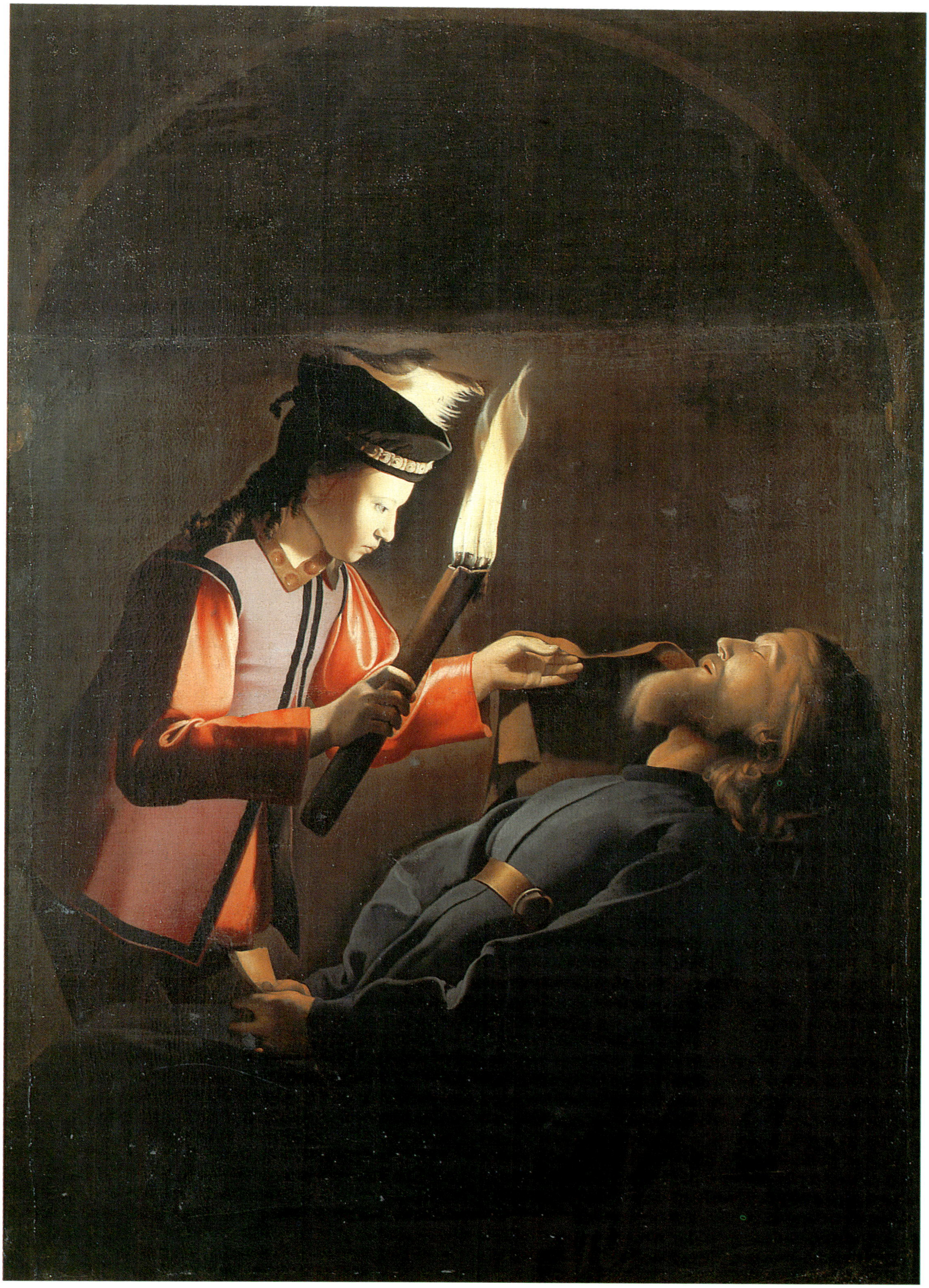

THE DISCOVERY OF SAINT. ALEXIS' BODY.
Nancy, Musée Historique Lorrain
158 × 115 cm.

wedding night, while his young bride was unfastening her tunic, Alexis re-covered his wife's breast, advised her to preserve her modesty, and gave her a gold ring and the belt he was wearing, asking her to keep them. He took ship for Laodicea. From there he went to Edessa, a Syrian town whose inhabitants treasured a portrait of Our Lord imprinted on a piece of linen. Alexis gave away all his clothes and, naked, began to beg under the porch of the church of Saint Mary in Edessa.

After seventeen years he left Edessa, landed in Ostia and made his way to his father's palace in Rome. No one recognised him. His father gave him alms.

For seventeen years he remained thus, unknown, in his father and mother's house. He ate the scraps left over from their meals. He lived under a staircase. When he felt death coming upon him, he asked for a stylus and wrote the story of his life on a scroll.

The Emperors Arcadius and Honorius and Pope Innocent were informed in a dream that there was a man of God in Euphormion's house. They sent their retainers to question the palace servants. By a process of elimination, it was soon decided that it could only be the beggar lying under the staircase. Torch in hand, a page leans over the saint,

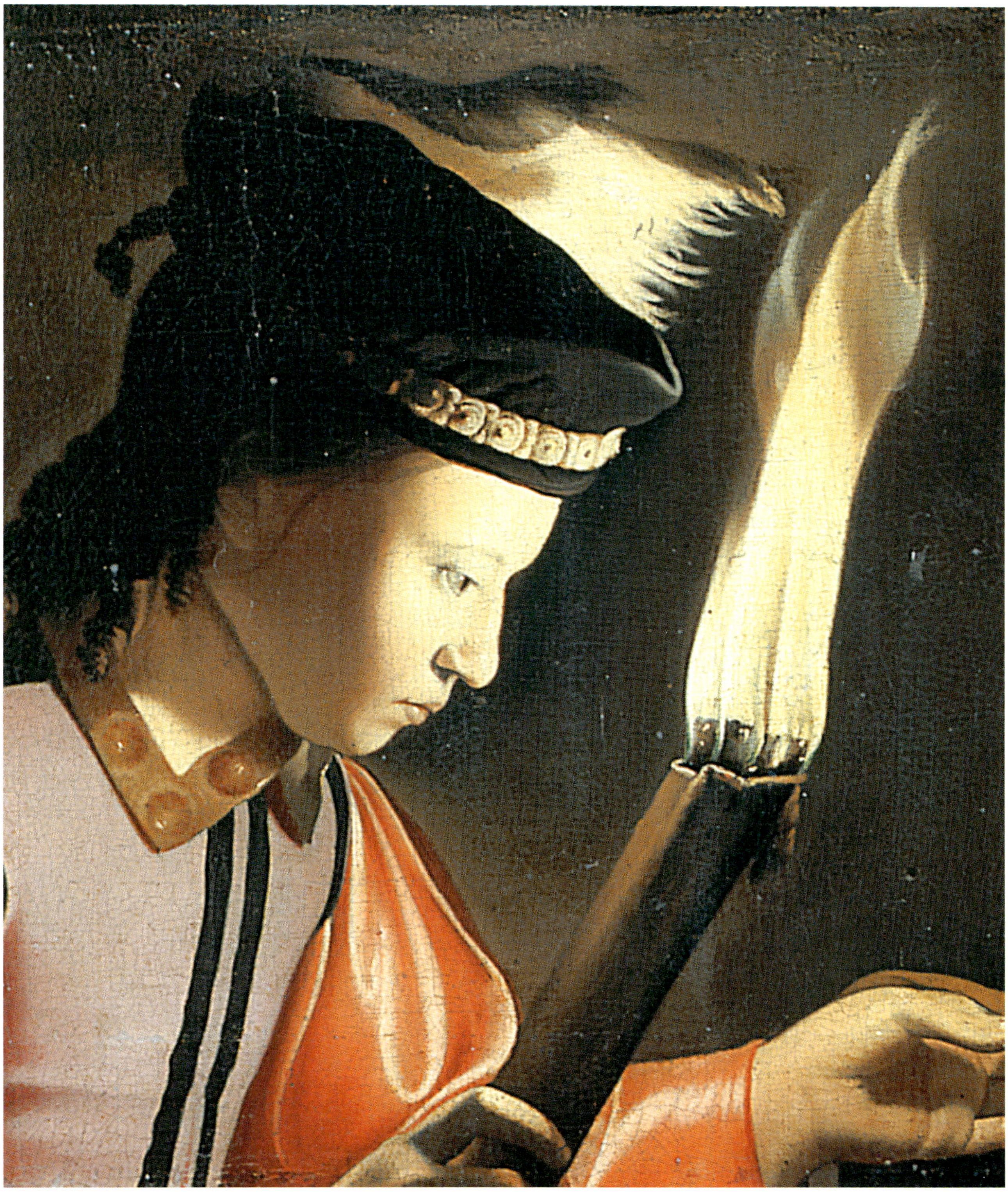

THE DISCOVERY OF SAINT. ALEXIS' BODY.
Nancy, Musée Historique Lorrain
detail.

already stiffened in death and holding Pope Innocent's letter in his hands. This is the most commonly accepted lesson.

In my opinion the page is holding out a piece of paper to determine whether Alexis is still breathing: this is the old rite of the Romans, who used to place a copper mirror over the lips of the dead man, calling him by his name three times. If the mirror did not mist over, the body could be consigned to the flames, after his image had been taken in hot wax.

And so I end this baroque suite of "images" of uncertain subjects, with the only painting whose meaning is definitely known: "Image Saint Alexis painted in 1648 for Monsieur de La Ferté".

The saint is holding the story of his life. The servant ascertains with a piece of starched linen that he is no longer breathing. The canvas is itself a spiral staircase. The saint is indeed the hero of chastity: his tight tunic is fastened by a slate-blue collar, his leather belt is pulled tight over the saint's chastity by an arrogant copper buckle.

The page with the torch is wearing a mauve doublet with blue ribbons, the sleeves of his jacket are bright red. His breeches are bluey-black. His collar is trimmed with yellow braid with orange bobbles. His toque is grey: it may well have been woven by Saint John of the Cross or his brother

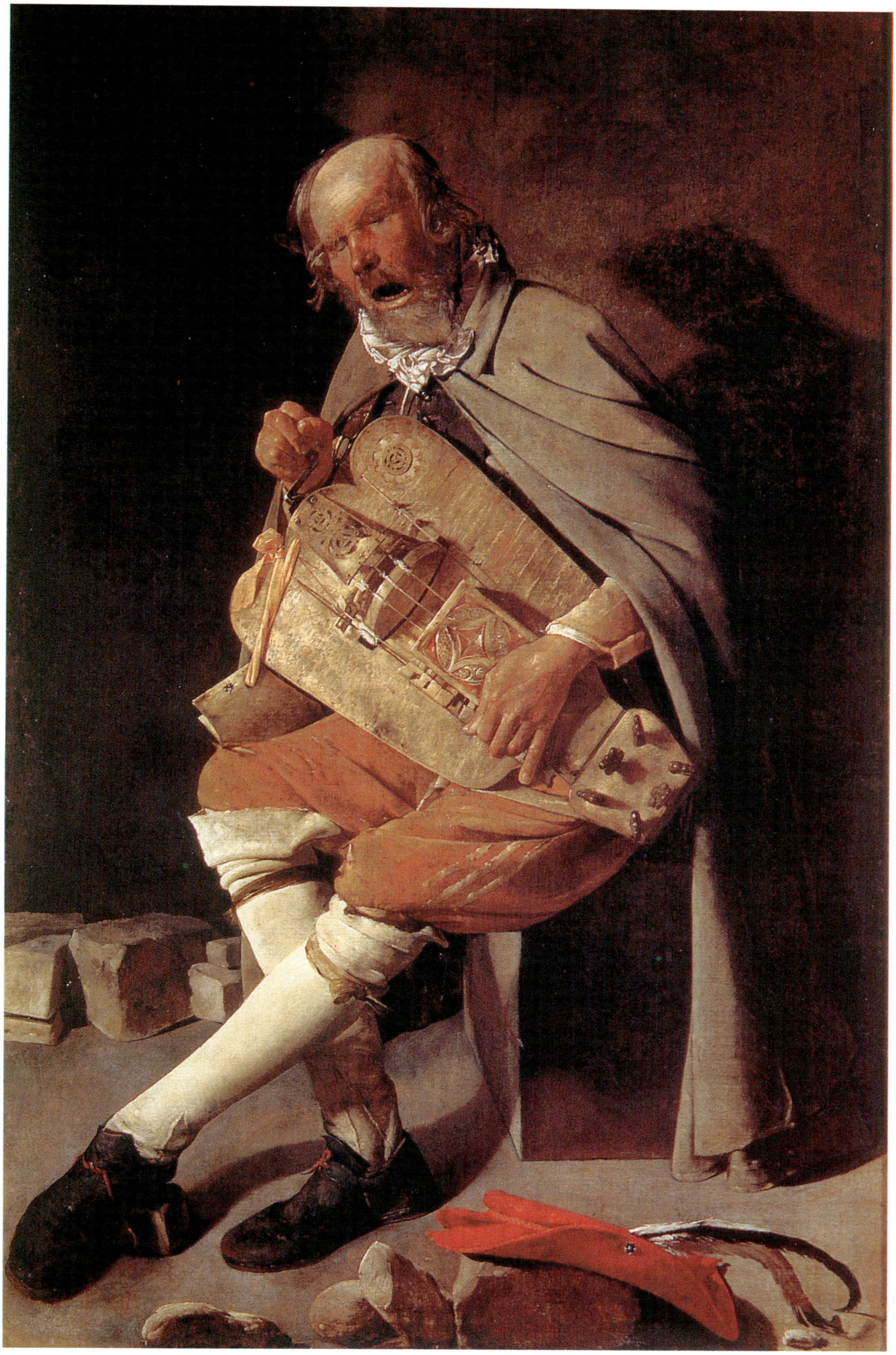

THE HURDY-GURDY PLAYER
(with hat).
Nantes, Musée des Beaux-Arts
162 × 105 cm.

Francisco de Yepes. When Euphormion and his wife went to the stairs to worship their son, they found him dead. Euphormion the prefect stretched out his hand to take the scroll his son was holding but could not get it out of his hand. The mother and father wept. The Pope and the two emperors ordered a stretcher to take the body to the church of Saint Boniface in Rome. This was on the sixteenth day of August in 398.

The child plays at the game of life and death with a bit of rag. He has no idea that he is in the presence of the first mendicant monk of ancient patrician Rome. He has no idea that he is in the presence of the man who, *par excellence,* is "He who is content to live unrecognised in the house of his father." A silent adolescent, seemingly on the verge of tears, is discovering death.

Georges de La Tour's son was no Alexis of Rome. He abandoned painting. He became a nobleman. He did not leave the patrician life for the shadow of a staircase. Etienne de La Tour was an Alexis who had become the prefect Euphormion. He became the lieutenant-general of the bailiwick of Lunéville. He did not have his father's works engraved. He did not write a memoir of his life. He obliterated the traces of plebeianism and the colourful memories of an artisan.

The great fire and the French soldiers had al-

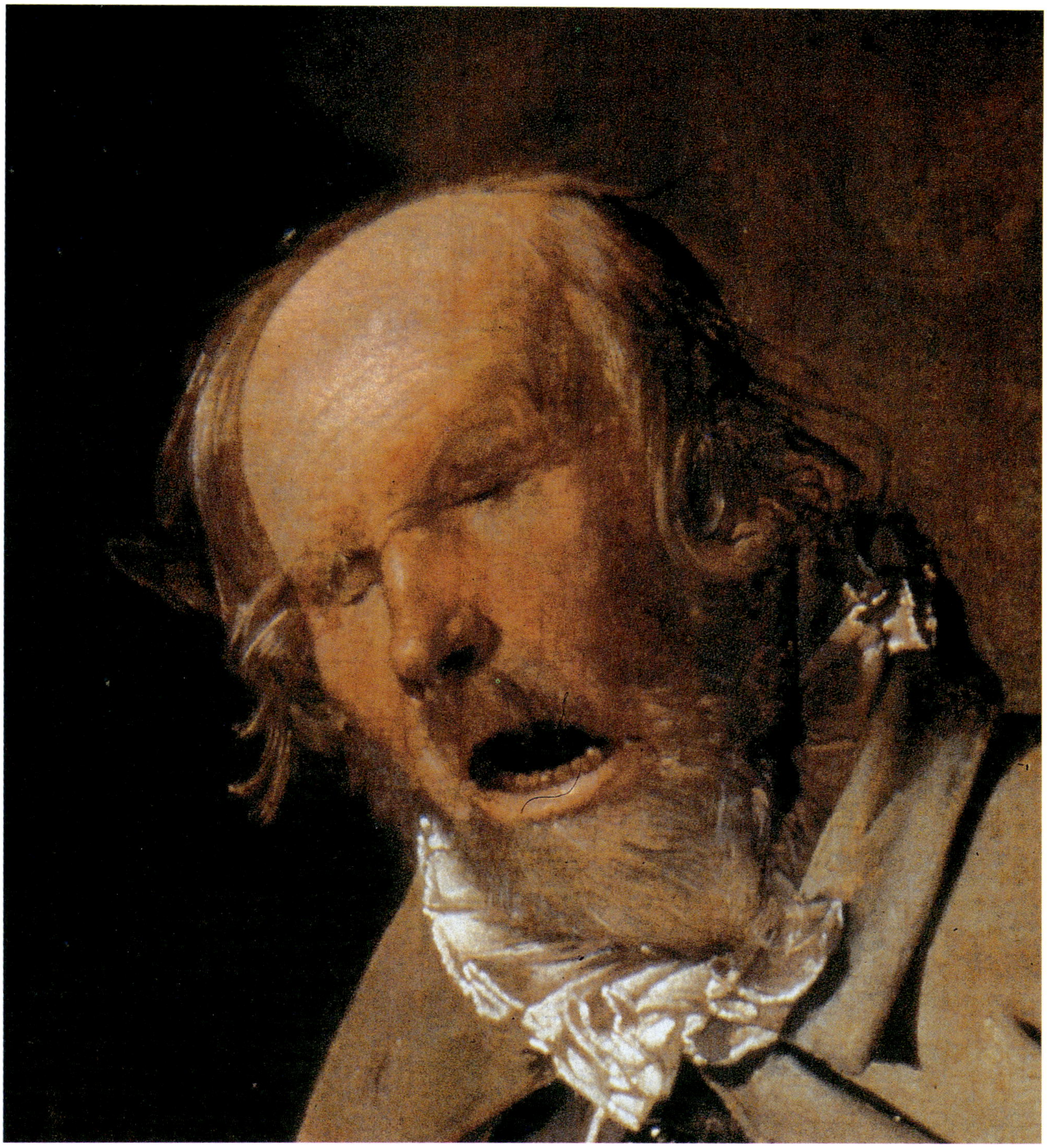

THE HURDY-GURDY PLAYER
(with hat).
Nantes, Musée des Beaux-Arts
detail.

ready burned more than half of everything Georges de La Tour had painted. Etienne de La Tour poured noble oil on this fire. Out of a production that must have counted between four and five hundred paintings there remained twenty-three originals, three engravings and two letters. And they had to wait for Stendhal and his disciple Taine to rediscover them.

One thinks of Jacques Esprit's remark: "I shall never be consoled for dying." In a world in which everything is moving towards death, death is the background. It is against this background that lone, insomniac women appear, and watchful children, and melting wax. The beauty of the gazes, the hands, the bodies, the lights that focus on them, the colours in which they are dressed, the doublets and the pattens, the hurdy-gurdies and the playing cards, the glasses and the books, the fingers reaching out — the beauty of all these is made of death. Beauty is the flame of a candle in sadness, in silver, in scorn, in solitude. In the night. A child's breath curves it; a puff of air threatens it; the final wind extinguishes it.

This is perhaps what the hurdy-gurdy player gives us to understand: "You who see the canvas that is under your eyes, you have only a blind man as a witness of your sight. This man who does not see you is screaming with pain: you do not hear

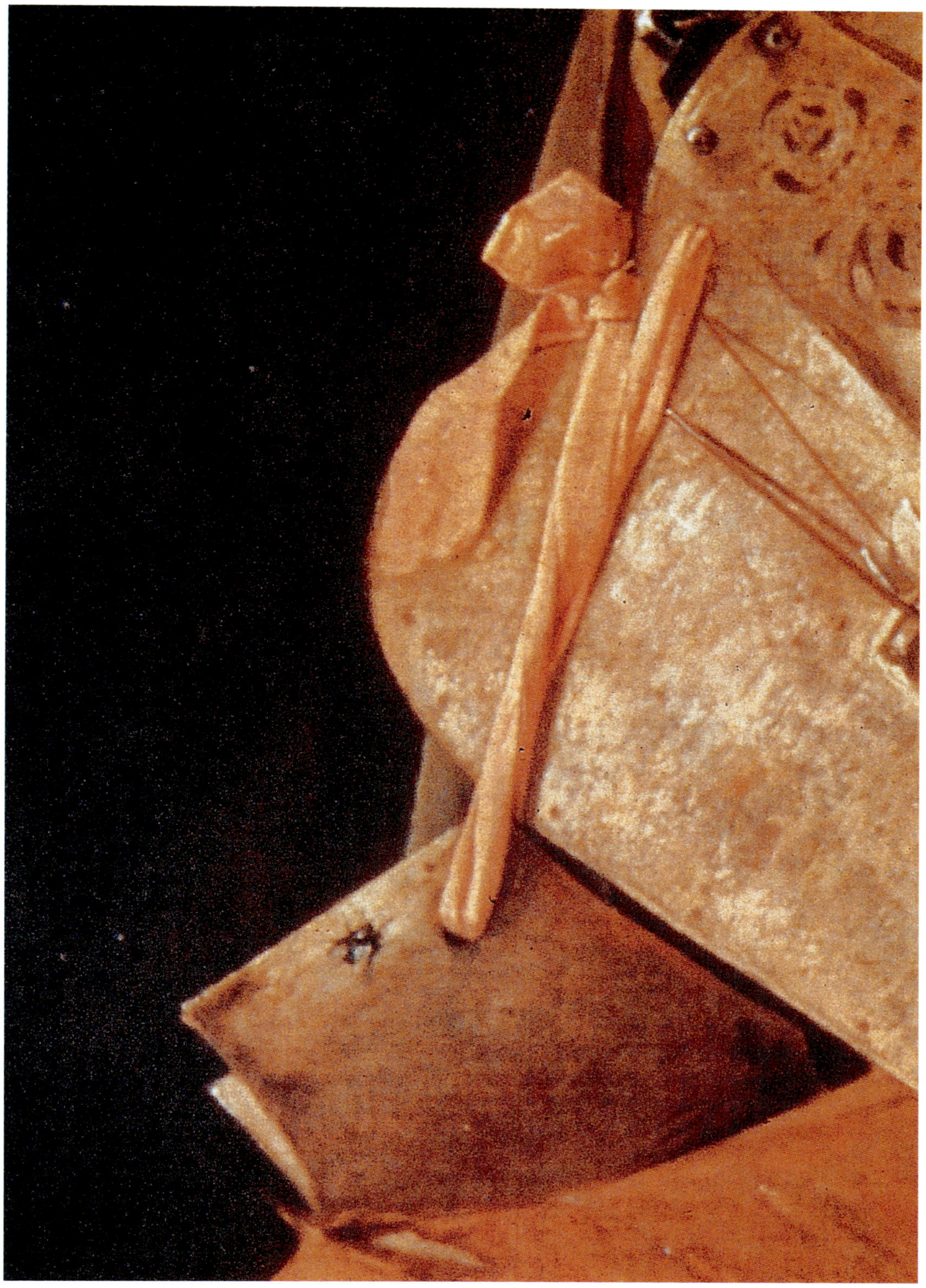

THE HURDY-GURDY PLAYER
(with hat).
Nantes, Musée des Beaux-Arts
detail.

him."

In one of his first canvases, like the disciples of Apelles, La Tour had painted a fly. His last painting is a flea. It is the haunting figure of the painted blind man, who sings (and who is silent), hirsute, poor. It is the theme of the "silentium loquens." Of the silent cry. The source of light is on the left, just outside. His cloak is grey, his stockings yellowish-white and torn, his shoes brown, their laces pink. A big bluebottle has settled, on the hurdy-gurdy.

It is the moth being burned by the candle. Like children at the moment of birth, they are more attracted by a passion for light than by the suffering that makes them scream.

For pagan Rome, it was not Alexis the son of Euphormion who had the most courageous role. In the eyes of the Fathers, it was Mutius Scaevola who gave proof of the greatest courage: he held his hand in the flame without flinching, and let it burn as if it had nothing to do with him. The closer one approaches the fire, the more one meditates on the fact that it amounts to the quantity of matter that is missing in its flame. What makes the flame brighter, the embers redder, the glow more luminous, is what becomes increasingly "nothing" in it. It is what is precipitated in order to become "nothing" in the heart of the furnace,

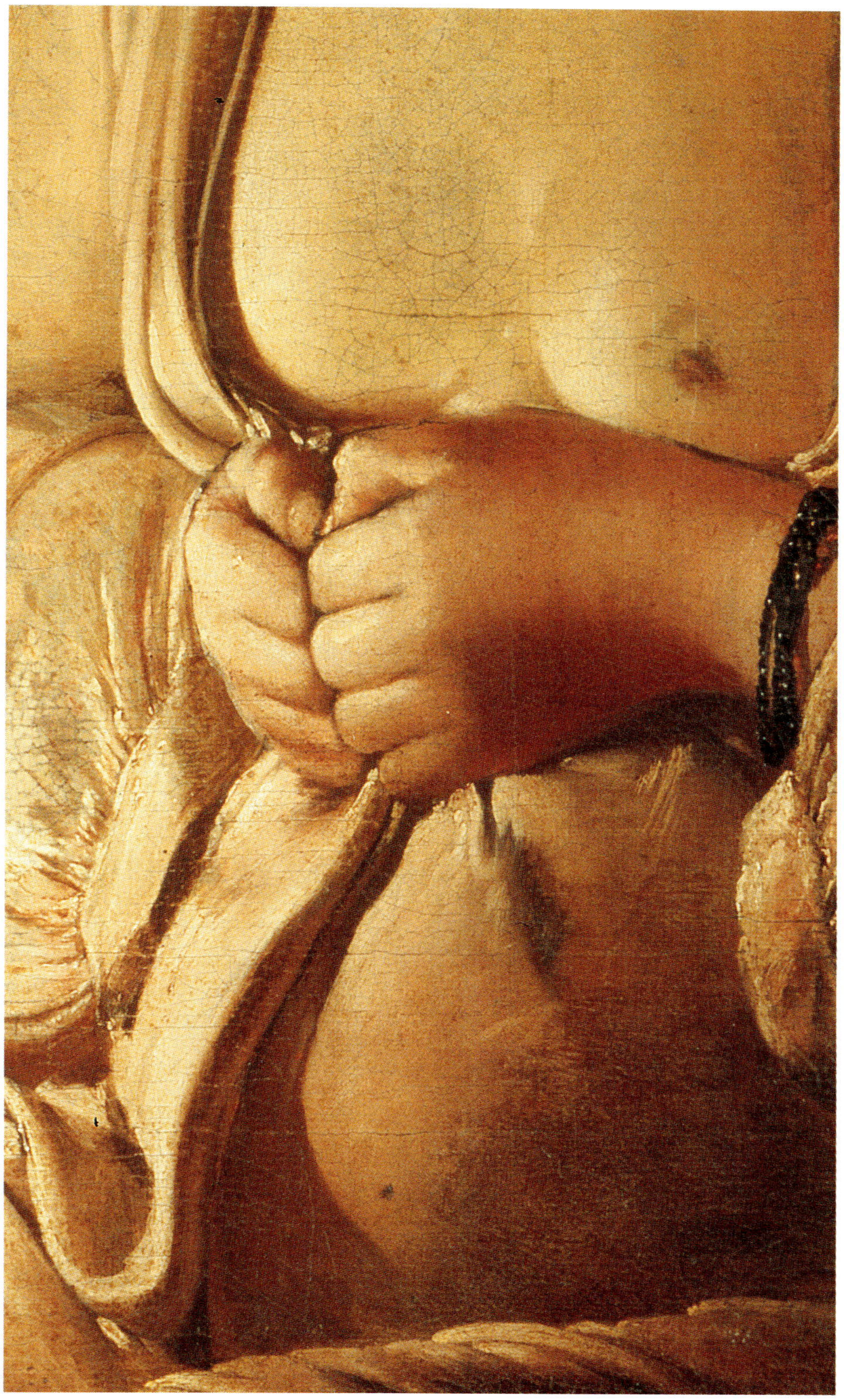

THE WOMAN AND THE FLEA.
Nancy, Musée Historique Lorrain
detail.

that collapses in it like an illusion, in the trembling, translucid air of the heat. It is this "nothing" that cries out in the crepitation. It is this "nothing" that is white in the heart of the flames; one cannot bring one's face close to it without screaming with pain. It is God.

THE WOMAN AND THE FLEA.
Nancy, Musée Historique Lorrain
detail.

GEORGES DE LA TOUR

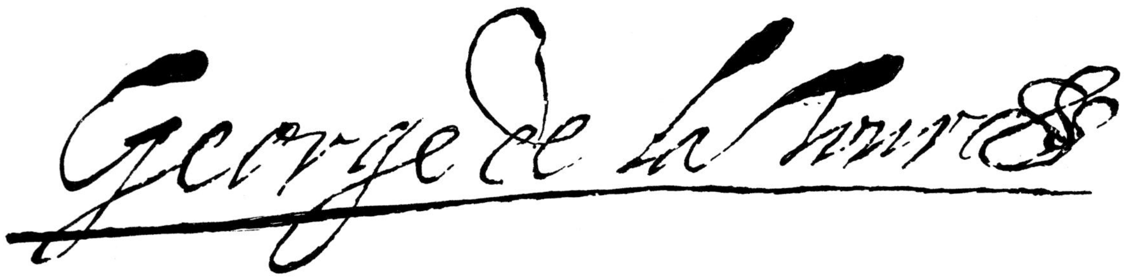

1593. Birth of Georges de La Tour at Vic-sur-Seille, a large market town in Lorraine under the bishopric of Metz. He was the second son of Jean de La Tour, baker by trade, and Sybylle Molian.

1593-1605. Georges de La Tour spent his childhood at Vic, but there are no documents covering the period, apart from christening certificates for his five brothers and sisters.

1605-1610. Very little is known about La Tour's education: it would appear that he served his apprenticeship as an artist in Lorraine, especially in Nancy where a number of painters, including Jacques Bellange and Claude Israel, had settled.

1610-1616. It is likely that La Tour traveled to Italy where he may have completed his education and discovered Caravaggio. Once again there is no evidence of this.

1616. Return to Vic.

1617. Georges de La Tour married Diane le Nerf, the daughter of the silversmith to the Duke of Lorraine and herself of noble birth. The marriage introduced him to local nobility.

1618-1619. Deaths of La Tour's father and father-in-law.

1619. Birth of La Tour's son Philippe.

1620. Georges de La Tour settled in Lunéville where the Duke built his château. Henri II of Lorraine bestowed letters of exemption on him conferring privileges similar to those of nobility.
In the same year he took Claude Baccarat of Lunéville as his apprentice.

1621. Birth of La Tour's second son, Etienne, the only one known to have been a painter.

1623-1624. Henri II of Lorraine acquired two of the artist's canvases.

1625-1631. Georges de La Tour led the life of a local squire. No documents exist on the work he produced at the time, but it appears that he received a large number of commissions. 1626, La Tour engaged another apprentice, Claude Roynet of Rémiremont.
His name began to appear in an increasing number of notarized documents, testifying to the esteem which he enjoyed.

1631-1635. War raged between France and Lorraine and the plague spread. Lunéville was pillaged and set alight, which explains the disappearance of the majority of La Tour's works prior to this period.
Nothing is heard of La Tour for a considerable time, which might be due to a voyage to Antwerp.

1636. Georges de La Tour engaged a new apprentice, his nephew François Nardoyen, who was to die of the plague shortly afterwards.

1638. Resumption of hostilities between France and Lorraine. Lunéville was ransacked and set alight.

1639. La Tour visited Paris, where he apparently intended to settle since he hired Guillaume Rué as his apprentice.
In December of that year he traveled to Nancy where he was cited for the first time as painter to Louis XIII.

1641-42. He became involved in litigation to ensute that his letters of exemption of 1621 would be respected.

1643. A new apprentice, Chrestien Georges, was hired.

1644. The beginning of a series of commissions from the town of Lunéville for the annual gift to the governor of Lorraine, Maréchal de la Ferté-Senectère. The first canvas was a nativity scene.

1645. Georges de la Tour signed and dated *"The Tears of Saint Peter"*, the first of his works to be attributed with certainty.

1646. His son Etienne was mentioned for the first time as a painter. He henceforth appeared to be associated with the work of his father.

1647. Etienne de La Tour married the daughter of a rich merchant of Vic.

1648. Death of La Tour's daughter Marie. Of ten children only two daughters and one son survived, Christine, Claude and Etienne.
Georges de La Tour took on a new apprentice, Jean Nicolas Didelot, whose contract stipulated that he also serve as a model to the painter.
The artist's paintings began to fetch substantial sums (1,700 francs and above).
La Tour was now wealthy and showed great interest in hunting, for which he even kept a pack.
He painted *"Image of Saint Alexis"* for Mr. de La Ferté.

1650. Birth of his grandson Jean Hyacinthe.
He signed and dated *"The Denial of Saint Peter"*.

1652. Georges de La Tour died on 30th January a few days after his wife and valet, casualty of an epidemic.

1654. His son Etienne in turn was given the title of painter to the King.
However, he gave up painting and was appointed Lieutenant de Guillage.

In 1670, Etienne de La Tour received his letters of ennoblement.

Georges de La Tour's works are exhibited in the following museums:

BELGIQUE

BRUSSELS
Musées Royaux des Beaux-Arts

FRANCE

ALBI,
Musée Toulouse-Lautrec.
BERGUES,
Musée municipal.
DIJON,
Musée des Beaux-Arts.
EPINAL,
Musée départemental des Vosges.
GRENOBLE,
Musée des Beaux-Arts.
LE MANS,
Musée Tessé.
NANCY,
Musée Historique Lorrain.
NANTES,
Musée des Beaux-Arts.
PARIS,
Bibliothèque Nationale,
Musée du Louvre.
REMIREMONT,
Musée Charles-Friry.
RENNES,
Musée des Beaux-Arts.

GERMANY

BERLIN-DAHLEM
Staatliche Museen, Gemäldegalerie

SWEDEN

STOCKHOLM,
Nationalmuseum.

UNITED KINGDOM

LEICESTER,
The Leicester Museum and Art Gallery.
MIDDLESBROUGH, TEESIDE (Yorkshire),
The Teeside Museum.

U.S.A.

CLEVELAND (Ohio),
The Cleveland Museum of Art.
DETROIT (Michigan),
Institute of Arts.
FORT WORTH (Texas),
Kimbell Art Museum.
LOS ANGELES, (California)
County Museum of Art.
MALIBU (California),
Paul Getty Museum.
NEW YORK,
Metropolitan Museum.
NORFOLK (Virginia),
Chrysler Museum.
SAN FRANCISCO,
De Young Memorial Museum.
WASHINGTON,
National Gallery.

USSR

LWOW,
Art Gallery.

By the same author

IN FRANCE

L'ÊTRE DU BALBUTIEMENT. 1969
Mercure de France

ALEXANDRA DE LYCOPHRON. 1971
Mercure de France

LA PAROLE DE LA DÉLIE. 1974
Mercure de France

MICHEL DEGUY. 1975
Seghers

ECHO, suivi d'EPISTOLÉ ALEXANDROY,
Le collet de buffle. 1975

SANG. 1976
Orange Export Ltd

LE LECTEUR. 1976
Gallimard

HIEMS. 1977
Orange Export Ltd

SARX. 1977
Maeght

LES MOTS DE LA TERRE, DE LA PEUR ET DU SOL. 1978
Clivages

INTER AERIAS FAGOS. 1979
Orange Export Ltd

SUR LE DÉFAUT DE LA TERRE. 1979
Clivages

CARUS. 1979
Gallimard

LE SECRET DU DOMAINE. 1980
Editions de l'Amitié

LES TABLETTES DE BUIS D'APRONENIA AVITIA. 1984
Gallimard

LE VOEU DE SILENCE. 1985
Fata Morgana

UNE GÊNE TECHNIQUE À L'ÉGARD DES FRAGMENTS. 1986
Fata Morgana

ETHELRUDE ET WOLFRAMM. 1986
Claude Blaizot

LE SALON DU WURTEMBERG. 1986
Gallimard

LA LEÇON DE MUSIQUE. 1987
Hachette

LES ESCALIERS DE CHAMBORD. 1989
Gallimard

ALBUCIUS. 1990
POL

KONG-SOUEN LONG, SUR LE DOIGT QUI MONTRE CELA. 1990
Michel Chandeigne

LA RAISON. 1990
Le Promeneur

PETITS TRAITÉS. 1990
Tomes I à VIII, Maeght

Is published in the United States by *Grove Press*

Photo credit: Jean Bazière: cover, p. 3, 5, 51 - Washington, National Gallery of Art: p. 7, 9, 11 - New-York, Metropolitan Museum of Art: p. 13, 15, 33 - Stockholm Nationalmuseum: p. 17 - Grenoble, Musée des Beaux-Arts: p. 19 - Albi, Musée Toulouse-Lautrec: p. 21 - Dijon, Musée des Beaux-Arts: p. 23 - Epinal, Musée Départemental des Vosges: p. 25, 59 - Rennes, Musée des Beaux-Arts: p. 27, 47, 49 - Lauros-Giraudon: p. 29, 45 - Hugo Maertens: p. 31, 35, 41, 43, 53, 69, 71, 73 - Fort Worth, Kimbell Art Museum: p. 37 - Musée du Mans: p. 39 - FR Grandi Opere Srl: p. 55, 57 - Gilbert Mangin: p. 61, 65, 67, 75, 77 - Giraudon: p. 63

© 1991 FLOHIC Editions 33 rue de la Brèche aux Loups 75012 Paris - Dépôt légal Avril 1991 - Imprimeur Campin, Tournai Belgique - Photocomposition ETNA Productions - I.S.B.N. 2-908958-00-7.